HIDDEN TREASURES

NORTHERN ENGLAND

Edited by Chris Hallam

First published in Great Britain in 2002 by
YOUNG WRITERS
Remus House,
Coltsfoot Drive,
Peterborough, PE2 9JX
Telephone (01733) 890066

Copyright Contributors 2002

HB ISBN 0 75434 084 8
SB ISBN 0 75434 085 6

FOREWORD

This year, the Young Writers' Hidden Treasures competition proudly presents a showcase of the best poetic talent from over 72,000 up-and-coming writers nationwide.

Young Writers was established in 1991 and we are still successful, even in today's technologically-led world, in promoting and encouraging the reading and writing of poetry.

The thought, effort, imagination and hard work put into each poem impressed us all, and once again, the task of selecting poems was a difficult one, but nevertheless, an enjoyable experience.

We hope you are as pleased as we are with the final selection and that you and your family continue to be entertained with *Hidden Treasures Northern England* for many years to come.

CONTENTS

Braithwaite CE Primary School, Keswick

Craig Robinson	19
Andrew Warren	19
Emma Little	20
Hannah Horsburgh	20
Josie Fisher	21
Emily Bunting	22
Dina Goodwill	22
Alice Sheppard	23
Matthew Lysser	24
Thomas Brown	24
Emma Atkinson	25
Ben Waite	25
Adam Robinson	26
Olivia Robinson	27
Sarah Sinclair	27

Brough Primary School, Kirkby Stephen

Sonia Hughes	28
Andrew Wilkinson	28
Thomas Walton	29
Claire Smith	29
Kerri Dickinson	30
Rebecca Lowery	30
Sophie Gelder	31
Lauren Betka	31
Jolie Souter	32
Jane Brunton	32
Hannah Ashcroft	33
Jo Jo Earl	33
Martyn Crowther	34
Alix Dent	34

Chilton Junior School, Ferryhill

Jordan Mallinson	35
Jack Wilson	35
Christian Thomsen	36
Jordan Wright	36

Harecroft Hall School, Seascale

Isla Frost-Pennington	72
Rickie Bewsher	72
Joanna Bentley	73
Kathryn Mrowicki	74
Becky Holliday	74
Rosanna Ponticelli	75
Dhriti Eapen	76
Thomas Cleave	76
Rebecca Morris-Eyton	76
Tasha Bradley	77
Marcus Brough	77
Alistair Mackintosh	78
Fraser Frost-Pennington	78
Emma Moore	79
Patrick Morris-Eyton	79
Laurence Gribble	80
Elspeth Block	80
James Cater	81

Hartside Primary School, Crook

Rebecca Anderson	81
Thomas Craggs	82
Anthony Conley	82
Liam Bailey	82
Jordan Paige Gent	83
Laura Hook	83
Helen Hodges	83
Michael Winter	84
Jessica Moore	84
Eamon Richardson	84
Laura Winter	85
Emma Louise Colling	85
Sarah Elizabeth Clarey	85
Paul Harvey	86
Sammie Lee Johnson	86
Jonathan Mason	86

Hensingham Junior School, Whitehaven

Linzi Nimmo	87
Emily Edgar	87
Heather Lewthwaite	87
James Linton	88
Stephanie Lowrey	88
Maryam Umar	89
Daniel Tyson	90
Jade Rogan	90
Catherine Edgar	91
Samantha Cannings	91

Heversham CE Primary School, Milnthorpe

Kayleigh Jones	92
Samuel Willacy	92
Emma Matthews	93
Jessica Rosser	93
Thomas Davies	94
Justine Walker	94
Jack Smith	95
Ashley Porter	95
Jonathan Hyman	96
Joanna Swinbank	96
James Hyman	97
Sophie Fishwick	98
Jamie Keatings	98
Liam Gannicliffe	99
Emily Crowder	100
Max Shaw	100
David Ely	101
Kirsty Tyson	101
Emma Chapman	102
Nick Hamer	102
Laurance Stannard	103
Matty Cummins	103
Douglas Parsons	104
Lauren Thompson	104
Laura Hamer	105

Maryport CE Junior School, Maryport

Mowden Junior School, Darlington

Plumpton School, Penrith

Ravenstonedale Endowed School, Kirkby Stephen

John Hall	175
Emma Norris	176
Ashley Ryan	176
Rebecca Scott	177
Sam Ruddy	177
Jenna Hall	178
Jake Smith	178
Jade Cunningham	179
Leanne Hoban	179
Kate Chorley	180
Simone Wilson	180
Martyn Wood	181
Catherine Steel	181
Emily Grima	182
Kerry Hall	182
Laura Skilling	183
Carrie Hall	183
Stuart Quinn	184
Jessica Taylor	184
Lucy Hoban	185
Stuart McCullock	185
Callum Doyle	186
Scott Auty	186
Tommy Wilson	186
Stacey Johnston	187
Megan Ranson	187
Robert Little	188
Nicholas Wood	188
Dean Norris	189

Shotton Hall Junior School, Peterlee

Josh Adamson	189
Ruth French	190
Dean Collings	190
Holly Venners	191
Jordan Wilson	191
Mathew Geldard	192
Stuart Robinson	192

Claire Barrass	193
Hannah Pearson	193
Glyn Pallister	194
Hayley Groves	194
Michelle Clark	195
Michelle Fullard	196
Kelsey Douglas	196
Jessica Errington	197
Laura Talbot	197
Carly Fishwick	198
Kate Gibson	198
Sophie Coldwell	199
Craig Benton	199
Fallon Hickman	200
Harley Ferguson	200
Annabelle Edwards	201
Michelle Keighley	201
Andrew Bell	202
Helen Clynes	202
Francesca Edwards	203
Craig Rhodes	203

Skelton Primary School, Penrith

Claire Donald	204
Gareth Hughes	204
Charlotte Miller	205
Amanda Jackson	206
Kerry Donald	206
Heather Blanshard	207
Katie Hughes	208
Freddie Stewart	209
Clemency Jolly	210

Storth CE Primary School, Milnthorpe

Ben Shaw	210
Jonathan Palmer	211
Aaron Marrs	211
Thomas McGregor	212

The Poems

CATS

Cats purr,
Have fur,
Don't fear,
Always here.
Cats hiss,
No bliss,
Always stalk,
Never walk.
Cats eat
Dog's meat,
By the door,
On the floor.
Cats tap
On flap,
Never fall
Off the wall.
Miaow!

Kerry Little & Nicola Bell (10)

IT WAS SO QUIET THAT I HEARD . . .

It was so quiet that I heard . . .
A princess letting down her hair,
A diamond shimmer in the sun,
A person weave gold cotton,
A crystal glitter in the moon,
A stringray flip in the clear blue water,
A rose lose a few petals,
A star float down the Milky Way,
A butterfly flutter away,
A fish curve in a wave,
A unicorn swirl its horn.

Rachel Jane Brizland (11)
Allonby Primary School, Maryport

Hidden Treasures - My Family

A mother who tries to keep me out of trouble,
Unfortunately keeps me wrapped in a protective bubble.
A dad who's always busy and also quite clever,
Whether or not he's cheerful it depends on the weather.
A sister who tells on me and drives me round the bend,
Who's OK sometimes though whose brain needs a mend.
A brother who's hyper, who messes up my stuff,
He's cute and cuddly though really - and he's my little bruv.
My grandad's into music, be it classical or jazz (but not pop!),
He's really quite artistic and I love him lots and lots.
My gran is a diamond, she really is no fool,
She's really, really kind - and she's just so cool.
My nana is a cookie who's always baking cakes,
Whether they're jam tarts or custard creams, she always knows just
what to make.
My uncle is a businessman, he sells Audi cars,
He's always driving from A to B, from Jupiter to Mars.
My auntie's wicked and she can even ice skate,
I dunno when I'll see her next, though I just can't wait.
My cousin Steph's really cool and she always emails me,
She's always out at parties and very brainy is she.
Laura is a real girl who's brainy and clever as can be,
She's ace at computers and very friendly is she.
Melissa is the quiet type even though she's really quite funny,
She really loves cartoons and her favourite is Bugs Bunny.
Monty is my bull-mastiff dog who sniffs and slobbers all day long,
Whilst he is a friendly dog, he unfortunately tends to pong!
That's my family!

Ashley Wood (10)
Barnard Castle CE Primary School, Barnard Castle

MY GRANDMA

My grandma is very kind and also very helpful,
  Whether things are good or whether they are very dreadful,
    She always thinks of others and never gives up
      And when I'm sad she cheers me up.
She had a stroke and got through that
  And Grandad's been so very annoying, she hasn't given him a bat,
    She has got a fake hip, teeth and knee,
      She has never really liked drinking, but she does like a cup of tea.
She is the best and I know that,
  Whether she's thin or whether she's fat,
    She talks to others and has a great mind
      And that's one of the reasons why I think she is one of a kind,
        She is loving and caring and never lets you down,
          So that's why I think she should be wearing a crown.

Zoë Wilkinson (11)
Barnard Castle CE Primary School, Barnard Castle

MY FLUFFY CAT, HENRY

My cat Henry is a fluffy white and ginger cat,
Whenever he is on his own he scratches the wall,
When people torment him he attacks your toes,
His fur is very loud, his fur is as fluffy as a teddy bear,
Sometimes he licks your hand when you stroke him,
He is a cute and fluffy cat, he used to be a kitten,
He is always purring, he is always sleeping because he is a lazy cat,
Henry always sleeps with his crocheted blanket,
He has lots of friends, there is Casper the kitten, Felix the cat,
                                        Laddie the dog,
He loves to look out of the window at other animals like mice and birds,
If the window is open he sticks his nose out into the fresh air.

Kelly Proffitt (10)
Barnard Castle CE Primary School, Barnard Castle

MY COUSIN IS . . .

My cousin is mad,
My cousin is insane,
My cousin is a pain,
My cousin is no picture frame.

> My cousin is a Barbie lover,
> My cousin is a crazy cover,
> My cousin is very strange,
> My cousin is no angel.

My cousin is round the bend,
My cousin, I can lend,
My cousin isn't cute
And my cousin is definitely not
Hidden treasure.

Abbie Dye (11)
Barnard Castle CE Primary School, Barnard Castle

THE HIDDEN TREASURE

In my mind Theo is a treasure
He is very kind and he never finishes work
He is a good footballer on and off the pitch
Sometimes he is fair and at times rough
Likes his hair stuck up, then again not
He is a big fan of Sunderland FC
Then again he plays football a lot
He lives in a pub on the end of Barney
He is not a good speller
Then at times he is a good story writer
At times he needs help with his work
He has lots of girls after him.

Jonathan Hedley (10)
Barnard Castle CE Primary School, Barnard Castle

IF

If my mum was an animal
She'd be a small squirrel;
Running freely though the forest
Not a care for anything or anyone.

If my mum was a monster (she sometimes is!)
She'd be big and strong;
Doing nothing but eating
All day long.

If my mum was a bird
She'd be a bluebird;
Flying swiftly and fast
Through the fluffy white clouds.

Phillip Woodward (10)
Barnard Castle CE Primary School, Barnard Castle

MY HIDDEN TREASURE

Since I've played the game,
My life's not the same,
Everything about it I love,
I pray for a dry, sunny day,
When to my match I can play.

I put on my kit
And jog about to keep fit,
I know that this is it,
I play with a passion,
I have my own fashion,
But football for me is all I can see,
Nothing to measure,
Football's my treasure.

Daniel Knight (11)
Barnard Castle CE Primary School, Barnard Castle

THE DOG!

The dog I know is one cool pup,
Jumping around, she'll never stop,
Wherever you go she'll follow you,
So watch out or she'll lick you!

Around the house she will run,
Running like a bullet from a gun,
I always laugh to see such joy,
As she gnaws on her squeaky toy!

She is like a queen's royal treasure,
You'll never find a dog like that,
Because she is always chasing . . .
Rats!

If you had a dog like that,
You'd love the gentle soul,
Beneath her soft and furry coat,
But you'll never find a dog like that.

Nicola Gargate (10)
Barnard Castle CE Primary School, Barnard Castle

MY SPECIAL FRIENDS

My first friend is Zoe,
She likes to go to the sea,
Sometimes she takes a friend,
Sometimes that is me.

My other friend is Alex,
She likes doing sport,
When she goes on holiday,
She goes to an airport.

My last friend is Loisea,
She was a bridesmaid with me,
We always meet up,
We are happy as can be.

Rachael Lee (10)
Barnard Castle CE Primary School, Barnard Castle

HIDDEN TREASURE

Hidden treasure everywhere,
They're everywhere you look,
They're in the washing,
In the bed,
They're quite common in books.

Hidden treasure everywhere,
As far as the eye can see,
They're in the bin,
Under the sofa
And in cups of tea!

Hidden treasure everywhere,
You as well can spot
They're in the garden,
Under the chair,
Also in flowerpots.

Hidden treasure everywhere,
Some are in disguise,
Look around
And you will see,
Trust me, you'll be *surprised!*

Anya Thomas (10)
Barnard Castle CE Primary School, Barnard Castle

PETS

First a cat,
Then a dog,
Now no cat.
We've got a fish,
No wait, another dog.
There's a hamster,
Now it's gone.
Lots of puppies,
Now only one.
We've got a budgie,
It's flown away.
Please, another pet, I pray,
Another hamster,
Puppies arrive,
Sell them all,
Then hamster dies.
Now three gerbils
And a fish,
Only two gerbils,
Please let them live.

Stephanie Poulter (10)
Barnard Castle CE Primary School, Barnard Castle

MY FAMILY

My brother is a freak
And my mum is a geek;
My dad is bad
And acts like a lad.

My grandpa is old
And my gran is gold;
My auntie is a pig
And my uncle doesn't jig.

My friends are cool,
They like to play pool;
My cousins love a duel,
Everyone's cruel!

James Tomlinson (10)
Barnard Castle CE Primary School, Barnard Castle

MY FAMILY

I wake up every morning,
My alarm clock goes *beep, beep,*
Then I tiptoe downstairs,
To take a little peep.

Mum's cooking the breakfast,
Dad's watching the news,
Both sisters are playing
With the Barbie dolls.

My dad walks towards me,
I leap up the stairs,
Look at all the bristle,
I get confused with bears.

Then comes Mum,
Somewhere along the line,
She's dreaming of a cottage,
With grapes by the vine.

Next comes my sister,
With a Barbie Jeep,
So I hide behind the sofa
And take another peep.

Alex Nicholson (11)
Barnard Castle CE Primary School, Barnard Castle

TIMOTHY, MY CAT

Where are you Tim?
I'm looking for you -
In the cupboard,
Down the loo,
Under the table,
Up the stairs,
On the bed,
Between teddy bears,
In the bath,
Having a laugh,
Under the bed,
On my head,
In a hat,
On the mat,
Back downstairs,
In front of the fire,
Oh Tim, you're there; on the chair!

Katie Welsh (10)
Barnard Castle CE Primary School, Barnard Castle

CATS

Cats are loving,
Cats are kind,
Cats eat mice, they don't mind.

Cats are fun,
Cats are quiet,
Cats are curled up in front of the fire.

Cats hate water,
Cats love sleep.

Lucy Brenkley (10)
Barnard Castle CE Primary School, Barnard Castle

MY HIDDEN TREASURE

Brothers

You'll never be Buzz Lightyear,
You'll never reach the stars,
You'll never be a fighter,
You'll never have a car,
You'll never be a prize,
You'll never grow that size,
You'll never get a friend
Who's not round the bend,
You never shut your mouth,
You can't tell west from south,
But you're still my little brother
And I'll always love ya,
But you'll always be a hidden treasure.

Rheanne Laybourn (10)
Barnard Castle CE Primary School, Barnard Castle

MY HIDDEN TREASURE

My dog Cass
Black with spots
He hates cats
He's a lazy bat
He thinks he's a book ripper
But really, he's a fur licker
He's also a wood chewer
Big fighter and a football lover
He's a wet dripper, friendly player
A fast runner and he's a dirt roller
He's my hidden treasure.

Sam Everett (10)
Barnard Castle CE Primary School, Barnard Castle

MY BEST FRIEND

I have a best friend,
Her name is Megan W,
She said that she has a friend,
Her name is Katie W.

Now Megan has a pal,
He is very silly and wild,
His name is Thomas W,
He is anything but mild.

If you want to see them,
Go to Barnard C,
Go north then east,
Then go down the MWT.

But if you're sensible,
I wouldn't go,
Not whilst Thomas stays,
But Megan is my best friend,
So I would go there anyways.

Kay Hadden (10)
Barnard Castle CE Primary School, Barnard Castle

BUSTER

A mass of glorious liver spots,
Surrounded by a cloud of white,
A tall handsome figure
And a personality so bright.

Chewing things is his game,
Always growing up,
I really do love
That glorious little pup.

A lovely Dalmatian,
Full of care,
If you wish to, you can stand and stare,
Maybe go close, if you dare.

If he doesn't like you,
You'll get a scowl,
Take another step
And he'll bark and growl.

Louise Ford (10)
Barnard Castle CE Primary School, Barnard Castle

MY DEMON BROTHER

My brother is a pain,
He really is insane,
He caught twenty rats and put them in a stew,
He's got birds and rabbits and now he's after you!

He froze his favourite pigeon
And fed it to the cat,
She ate and ate and ate it,
She got really fat!

He stole the air rifle
And aimed it at the trifle,
The cream and fruit were splattered
And the bowl, extremely battered!

But most of all I'd like to say,
My brother is insane
And now to end the poem,
You wouldn't like to know him!

Ross Gargett (10)
Barnard Castle CE Primary School, Barnard Castle

TV

You, you are a box, perfect square,
  You, you are chocolate-brown,
    You, you are cyber clear,
      You, you are so clear as crystal,
        You, you are like a member of the family,
          You, you are able to show what's on
            You! You are my TV!

          You, you will never be complete,
        You, you will never get up and walk,
      You, you will never blink,
    You, you will never be a relative,
  You, you will never have feeling,
You, you are my TV!

Dominic Cooper (10)
Barnard Castle CE Primary School, Barnard Castle

MY HIDDEN TREASURE

Smooth black coat,
Black as night,
Playfully chewing on the comfy chairs,
He's a naughty little tyke.

Extremely speedy runner,
Chasing me everywhere,
Never ever stops,
He's a playful little thing.

Every day he wants to play with me,
Never leaves me alone,
That's why he is so special to me,
That's my puppy, Ollie.

Stephanie Day (10)
Barnard Castle CE Primary School, Barnard Castle

DOGS

Dogs are cool
And sometimes scary,
Dogs are cuddly
And very hairy.

Dogs are fast
And never miss anything,
Dogs are different,
Sometimes good or bad.

Dogs are powerful,
So never get on the wrong side of them,
Dogs drink fast
And eat really quickly.

Martin Oates (10)
Barnard Castle CE Primary School, Barnard Castle

THE TRAMP

There's a tramp, yes a tramp
And he sits in the cellar,
I've thought of telling Mum,
But I don't want to be a teller.

He settled by the window,
I gave him a blanket or two,
He's been there ever since,
I just don't know what to do.

My mum and dad are really posh,
They act like king and queen,
But I like to take risks
And live life to the extreme.

Tom Maine (10)
Barnard Castle CE Primary School, Barnard Castle

MY BED

My bed is warm,
My bed is calm,
My bed adventures into the jungle,
My bed makes boulders rumble.

My bed can make snowflakes fall,
My bed surrounded by castle walls,
My bed is fit for a king,
My bed gives the enemy a sting.

My bed can make rockets sprint into space,
My bed is just the best place,
My bed transports me into the deepest mine,
My bed can stop time.

My bed destroys panic,
My bed is a distant planet,
My bed is brill,
My bed sits in the corner still.

Robert Lumsdon (10)
Barnard Castle CE Primary School, Barnard Castle

HIDDEN TREASURE

When we think of Treasure Island,
We think of pirate ships,
Of golden sands and palm trees
And sunny summer trips.

The rock pools and the dark caves,
Where we explore at leisure,
Of mums and dads relaxing,
Enjoying warmer weather.

We're eating lots of ice cream
And having lots of fun,
Digging on the sandy beach
And playing in the sun.

But what we enjoy most of all,
From what we get most pleasure,
Is hoping that one day we'll find
Some buried pirate treasure.

Emma Smith (10)
Barnard Castle CE Primary School, Barnard Castle

MY HIDDEN TREASURE

Into the door
And over the carpet
Up the stairs
And into the toilet
Around the corner
And into my room
On my bed
And under my pillow
You'll find a key!
Look ahead, you will see
A set of drawers
Sitting there waiting
Use the key and open it carefully
Open the lid and look inside
You will find wondrous things like:
A crystal necklace from old Auntie Freda
And a couple of photos of silly Uncle Tom
Not forgetting the old china doll from my dear old father
All these are my hidden treasures!

Nicole Brown (10)
Barnard Castle CE Primary School, Barnard Castle

DOLPHINS IN THE WAVES

Jumping out of the waves,
Hunting for food,
Diving in the deep ocean,
To reveal what was untold,
Whirling, splashing all around,
Making a beautiful, tuneful sound,
Swirling, while fish live their lives,
In silver-grey, reflecting light,
The dolphin shows peace and delight.

Swimming through a sunken wreck,
Doing what they do best,
Gliding through the seaweed deep,
Going either north, east, south or west,
Diving, turning in ships wakes all their days,
But then it's night-time and all is quiet,
So they sink to the bottom to have a brief rest,
The dolphins rest and play throughout their lives,
Living, dying and bringing joy is their bequest.

Zoë Mitchell (10)
Barnard Castle CE Primary School, Barnard Castle

MY . . .

My brother is a vampire
My dad is a fly
My mum is a butterfly, as sweet as pie
My nana is a grasshopper
My grandma is a giraffe, as tall as a tree
My grandad is a rugby player, as strong as a rhino
My uncle is a pig, as smelly as can be
My auntie is a lion, brown as a door.

Jack Hutchinson (10)
Barnard Castle CE Primary School, Barnard Castle

WINTER'S HERE

Winter's here, as cold as ice,
The freezing cold is not very nice,
The snow is falling on the hills,
Icicles hang from the window sill,
The cold wind blows through the thin leaves,
It really is a crisp, cold breeze,
Sitting inside watching a warm log glow,
I'd rather be in here, than out in the snow.

Luke Tallentire (10)
Barnard Castle CE Primary School, Barnard Castle

THE MAN FROM HEAVEN

There was a man from Heaven
Who started to sing in Devon
He sang a wrong note
Stepped on a stoat
That silly old man from Heaven.

Craig Robinson (10)
Braithwaite CE Primary School, Keswick

LIMERICK

There was an old man from Devon
Who swallowed a hairclip from Heaven
He went to his wife
To ask for a knife
That poor old man from Devon.

Andrew Warren (10)
Braithwaite CE Primary School, Keswick

THE SEA

I am Sea
I call to you to tell
Of gifts that I use well

I run forever up and down the shore
To make sure in fun, you get a lot more

In me you throw balls and swim
Until the sun is shyly dim

But some people aren't very good
And throw things that they think they should

But they throw things ever so bad
Which makes me ever so mad

But I shall always fight
For what is oh so right

So you can play and have fun
And I can lie back in the sun.

Emma Little (11)
Braithwaite CE Primary School, Keswick

THE YOUNG WOMAN FROM BRAITHWAITE

There was a young woman from Braithwaite
Who fancied a boy from Thornthwaite
They danced all night
And ended with a fight
That young woman from Braithwaite.

Hannah Horsburgh (11)
Braithwaite CE Primary School, Keswick

MY CAT

My cat's a schizophrenic
A real Jeckyl and Hyde
He has two different personalities
I know which one I prefer

At home he is sweet, soft and cuddly
So cute and loveable .
And sleeps like a little darling
On my bed all day

When I stroke him, my cat purrs
Like a gigantic steam engine
And when I play table tennis
He's always there, acting ball boy

But . . .

When my cat goes out at night
He turns into a stalking tiger
Catching innocent birds and mice
And leaves remains on the back doorstep

Sometimes he loses track of time
And goes off for two-week breaks
He gets into fights with foxes and other cats
Then tears up the back door mat

My cat's a schizophrenic
A real Jekyll and Hyde
But I love him all the same
My schizophrenic cat.

Josie Fisher (11)
Braithwaite CE Primary School, Keswick

NIGHT

The sun sets
And the moon rises
The animals
And
People go
To sleep
Everything is
Silent
So
Peaceful
An owl
Hoots a
Ghostly sound
In the
Trees
Peering
From a
High branch
A fox is
Hunting
On the farm
In a
Moonlit
Sky.

Emily Bunting (11)
Braithwaite CE Primary School, Keswick

FRIENDS

Friends, friends, good friends
Sometimes fall out
Sometimes not
Friends, friends, best friends

Friends, friends, wonderful friends,
Kind as can be
As great as can be
Friends, friends, funky friends.

Dina Goodwill (10)
Braithwaite CE Primary School, Keswick

SELL FOR ANYTHING!

1920's grandad for sale,
Needs a few repairs,
No cuts or bruises,
Used to be in the RAF,
Got loads of medals,
Will sell for anything!

1989 high-voltage dog,
Beware, explosive fangs,
Needs regular exercise,
Preferably five miles a day,
MOT next year,
Will sell for anything!

1997 sister for sale,
Beware of flying toys,
Plays with Barbies
All day long,
Please take her off my hands,
Will definitely
Sell for anything!

Alice Sheppard (11)
Braithwaite CE Primary School, Keswick

EPITAPHS

Here lies the body
Of Danny Doom,
He discovered a bomb
And it went *boom!*

Here lies the body
Of Mr Fleep,
He was eaten
By a sheep.

Here lies the body
Of Andy May,
He burped so strong
His wife blew away.

Here is the body
Of Mrs Tee,
She was stung
By a killer bee.

Matthew Lysser (9)
Braithwaite CE Primary School, Keswick

SPROCKET AND HIS ROCKET

There was a young man called Sprocket
Who invented a spaceship rocket
The rocket went bang
His pants went twang
And his wig ended up in his pocket.

Thomas Brown (10)
Braithwaite CE Primary School, Keswick

SCHOOL'S OUT

Chatter, chatter
Boys flatter
Wriggle, wriggle
Girls giggle
Paper chain
Toy crane
Apple core
Chalky floor
Grey dress
What a mess
Hinges creak
Girls shriek
Teachers shout
School's out.

Emma Atkinson (11)
Braithwaite CE Primary School, Keswick

SUMMER

The summer is hot
The children play
The birds are singing
And the feelings are high
The days are long
The nights are short
But now summer's over
The children go indoors
The rain is pouring
And the feelings are cold.

Ben Waite (11)
Braithwaite CE Primary School, Keswick

WHERE HAS ALL THE MONEY GONE?

Europe our destination,
It was very sunny,
But oh we had problems,
Trying to spend the money.

In Spain with the peseta,
You can't even buy a potata.

In Portugal spending the escudo
Is as hard as solving Cluedo.

In Norway the workers all moan,
If you try to offer them krone.

In Finland offering markka to Fins,
Was as much good as throwing them in bins.

Francs, 'No thanks,'
In Belgium, Luxembourg and France.

In Austria we were willing,
But no one would take our shilling.

In Ireland our waiter grunts,
'I'm sorry, we can't take punts.'

It was very hot in Greece,
The drachma being as good as a fleece.

In Italy, Aunt Vera,
Was left with millions of lira.

Arriving in Germany after dark,
'We're hungry, will anyone please take our mark.'

But one thing that I do know,
Next year we'll take the Euro!

Adam Robinson (10)
Braithwaite CE Primary School, Keswick

ELEPHANTS

Elephants, elephants come in all different sizes,
Elephants, elephants, how huge you are
With your great big tusks
And your great big feet

Elephants, elephants, how grey you are
Elephants, elephants, wonderful you are
With your great big trunk
And your tiny little tails

Elephants, elephants, with your long legs
Elephants, elephants, can see a lot
With your lovely grey ears
As well as your dirty toenails.

Olivia Robinson (10)
Braithwaite CE Primary School, Keswick

THE SHADOW MONSTER

Sssh . . . I hear the shadow monster in the corridor,
I hear his heavy footsteps on the landing floor.

He creeps through the darkness to frighten you at night,
Although you cannot see him, he will give you a fright!

When you're in your bedroom and dark is all around,
That's when the shadow monster comes out and spoils the silent sound.

But when the night is over and it's morning again,
The shadow monster hides away, but he's still got your life to gain!

Sarah Sinclair (10)
Braithwaite CE Primary School, Keswick

MY FRIEND

My friend is cool
But sometimes stupid
With brown hair and blonde streaks
In her hair

She can be silly
And sometimes gets on my nerves
She's called Jane
With spooky brown eyes

With hair like the sun
And eyes like mud
She's a lot bigger than me
And she's my best friend.

Sonia Hughes (10)
Brough Primary School, Kirkby Stephen

MAN U

Man U are the best team
In the whole wide world
They win some
They lose some
They draw some too
Their rivals are Liverpool
They've lost to them
The last four times
But still
They are the best team
In the whole wide world.

Andrew Wilkinson (11)
Brough Primary School, Kirkby Stephen

THE TRAIN AND BUS

One fine day, we went on a trip, alone,
When our coach
Got to where we were going,
The bus broke down.

We had to wait for the other bus
To take us back,
So, for the rest of the day,
We went on the train.

To the other end of the line, and back,
We went again,
Our bus was waiting to take us
Back home again.

Thomas Walton (9)
Brough Primary School, Kirkby Stephen

ALIENS

Aliens, aliens
All over the place
They rule all over space

Will we find them
Yes or no?
We'll have to have a go

Yes, yes, yes
Green and flubbery
What is it . . .?

Claire Smith (11)
Brough Primary School, Kirkby Stephen

ON THE FARM

When I wake up in the morning
I'm always yawning
I can hear the cows
Getting ready to be milked
I can hear the sheep chewing on the grass

When I tiptoe down the stairs
Mum's always there
I enjoy my breakfast
I run down to the cellar to put my wellies on
My dad is milking the cows
I run to help him

Time to round the sheep in
I jump on the red quad bike
And start doing my job
The day is over now
Time to go to bed.

Kerri Dickinson (11)
Brough Primary School, Kirkby Stephen

THE BALLOON

Up, up, up and away
Watch the balloon float away
Up in the sky
Watch it flying high
People trying to catch it
Little girl crying
They all want the balloon
Then . . . *pop!*

Rebecca Lowery (9)
Brough Primary School, Kirkby Stephen

THE COUNTRYSIDE

The countryside is where I like best
I visit there as a guest
The green trees rustle
And white sheep bustle
All around their grassy spaces

I sit somewhere
And stroke a hare
I look back at the farmhouse
I make a home for a field mouse
With half a tennis ball and some laces

I watch the moon late at night
The sheep lie down, just in sight
I realise it's time to go
I say goodbye, but I know
I'll play chase, but tomorrow . . .

Sophie Gelder (10)
Brough Primary School, Kirkby Stephen

SADNESS

I hear the news that my great-grandfather has died
My great-grandfather lives in a beautiful place
A better place than our Earth
Someday I will meet him, but not today
My great-grandfather still lives on in my heart
My mum's heart and my family's heart
But I still miss my great-grandfather.

Lauren Betka (10)
Brough Primary School, Kirkby Stephen

GADGETS

Widescreen TV
Now that's what I like
Listening to the CDs on the hi-fi
Mobile phones
Have you got one?
I haven't had mine very long

PC
Surfing on the net
The best gadget yet
Game Boy Advance
Purple or clear blue?
I'll get one before you.

Jolie Souter (10)
Brough Primary School, Kirkby Stephen

THE SCHOOLGIRL!

My friend is called Sonia,
Her hair is bright blonde,
She has three holes in her ears.

She sticks studs in her lugs
And has goodness knows
How many freckles on her face.

With bright seashore-blue eyes,
She goes to school
On a rickety white bus.

Jane Brunton (9)
Brough Primary School, Kirkby Stephen

AT THE SEASIDE

At the seaside
By the gushing tide
I see the seagulls
Flying by

Where the sun shines
It's nice and bright
It gives off
Lots of light

By the cliffs
Where the rocks are stiff
The birds nest quietly
At the seaside.

Hannah Ashcroft (10)
Brough Primary School, Kirkby Stephen

CHESTNUT HORSE

I hear a whinny and what could it be?
A beautiful tail swishing in the breeze.
Its head held high, galloping softly,
Chestnut coat, gleaming in the sun.
I let out a whistle,
It gallops up to me.
I feel its soft muzzle against my cheek.
My baby brother starts to cry,
It gallops into the horizon.

Jo Jo Earl (11)
Brough Primary School, Kirkby Stephen

HIDDEN TREASURE

Go and get your shovels and pickaxes,
We're going to find hidden treasure,
We have a map that's so old.

It is near the caves, after two days
We get there, looking at the map,
It says ten steps forward

From the big standing stone. Five steps left
From the waterfall, then nine steps
Forward from the round

Stone circle. Then, the last three steps and
We are at the cross. We start digging,
Then find the hidden . . .
Treasure.

Martyn Crowther (10)
Brough Primary School, Kirkby Stephen

SNOW

The snow glistens like a ground of diamonds
It is as white as any white snowdrop
It is freezing cold, but I love it
You make snow angels and they fly away
You make snowmen and they chat to you
You can have a snowfall fight
Now the snow is starting to melt
I say goodbye to the snowman
Now I am bored every day
Very, very bored . . .

Alix Dent (10)
Brough Primary School, Kirkby Stephen

SCROOGE

Have you heard of a man called Scrooge?
He was greedy, selfish and very, very rude
He counted his money and gave a pittance of a pay
People didn't ask him the time of day
Marley's ghost appeared one night
And gave Scrooge a terrible fright

Visited by ghosts from future, present and past
He wondered how long this would last
Future ghost showed him his fate
For change old Scrooge must not wait
Next morn' when he had awoken
That mean old streak had been taken.

Jordan Mallinson (11)
Chilton Junior School, Ferryhill

AN F1 POEM

Michael is looking for 3 titles in a row
Kimi is now going for McLaren
The fastest speed is made by Ralph at 197 mph
Ralph has won 5 races
There are 17 races in 1 season
Hakkinnen has left McLaren
Visit ITV-F1.com or
Get F1 racing or get
Auto Sport magazine
Arrows have not won any titles
Prost has not won any titles
Minardi have not won any titles
Everybody's looking forward to 2003!

Jack Wilson (9)
Chilton Junior School, Ferryhill

HIDDEN TREASURE

Hidden treasure, hidden treasure
People need the exact measure
Pirate ships everywhere
You are never to glare

Smelly swamps and ugly trees
You need a lot of keys
Lots, lots and lots of jewels
People carry lots of tools

Looking carefully at the map
Tools hanging from a strap
Finally finding the treasure spot
Digging, sweating, mind it's hot

Here comes the treasure chest
All are working at their best
Lock is open: look here
Let's celebrate and cheer!

Christian Thomsen (9)
Chilton Junior School, Ferryhill

THE UNIVERSE

The universe
Never gets worse
And never seems to reverse
'Who invented the universe?'

The Earth is our home,
It doesn't seem to feel of foam,
From a satellite we look like a gnome,
'Who invented our home?'

The sun is very hot,
That's what I never forgot,
It never seems to rot,
'Who invented the sun, so hot?'

The planet Saturn,
Never seems to flatten,
It doesn't seem to matter,
'Who invented Saturn's rings flatter?'

Jordan Wright (9)
Chilton Junior School, Ferryhill

SPLASH'S DANCE

There she goes
Gliding through the water
Dancing with the waves
Chasing the sun-kissed crest of the surf

Leaping for the sky
Trying to catch the burning sun
She shows off
Splishing and splashing

She calls for her friends
They play chase through the waves
Zigging and zagging
Twisting and turning
As they swim off to touch the setting sun
And wait for another day.

Zoe Keenan (8)
Chilton Junior School, Ferryhill

CHRISTMAS CHEER

25th of December,
All the decorations are up,
All the presents are under the tree,
And the turkey is in a pot.
People singing
And we are playing games.
In a minute we are going to
Party all day.
My dad is going through the gate.
Carol singers are here
Singing all different Christmas songs
And friends are calling
Mum's bawling . . .
And brothers annoy each other.

Ross Exelby (9)
Chilton Junior School, Ferryhill

HIGH FORCE

The water's flowing
The wind is blowing
It's really high
And the water flows by
Falling, falling to the ground
Making such a loud, loud sound
Never stopping
Always dropping
Plunging, plunging ever down
Rocks clashing round and round
Foaming white
Both day and night.

Ashleigh Denton (11)
Chilton Junior School, Ferryhill

SEA

The sea is crashing
The sea is splashing
The weather is rough
And boats sail tough
The waves burst
The sea has been cursed
How bad can it get?
It's just started yet
He shouts, 'Help!'
When he's all by himself
There's a lifeboat ahead
He could be dead
Whether rain or shine
He will be fine.

Annie Mann (10)
Chilton Junior School, Ferryhill

HIGH FORCE

The water which falls 70 feet
Clashes and crashes against the rocks
It foams and steams
Down
  Down
    Down
     Down
Plunging into the water
As the rapids begin to ebb and flow
As the cola plunges over the fall.

Oliver Thomsen (11)
Chilton Junior School, Ferryhill

THE SEA

Deep and dark and blue and green
The sea is the best place I have been
I jump right in and hold my breath
And swim around its scary depths
I play with dolphins all the day
And dive with whales down in the bay
I watch out, though, for Mr Shark
Hiding in the sea so dark

One day I swam down to a wreck
And walked along the wooden deck
And dug around until I found
Gold and jewels scattered around
I put them in a bag I had
And took them to my mum and dad
They couldn't speak when they saw
The treasure that I brought ashore

Best though, was the day that I
Asked a killer whale for a ride
I grabbed on to his jet-black fin
And very fast, began to swim
He went so fast it made me scared
I shouted, 'Stop,' he never heard
I let out a gigantic scream
And woke in bed, it was a dream.

Rosemary Tyas (8)
Chilton Junior School, Ferryhill

WOLF

Wolf began,
He took the roaring of the wind,
The snarl of the tiger,
The growl of thunder
And made his voice.

For his coat,
He took the black of night,
He took the whiteness from the clouds,
He took the greyness of mist.

From the wilderness,
He took the prowl of a hunter,
He took the darkness of a shadow
For his walk.

Then at night,
Wolf took the blackness of space,
The brilliance of the moon
To make his eyes.

Cutting knives
Went into the sharpness of his teeth
And for their shape,
He took the points of a star
And wolf was made.

Marc Shaw (11)
Chilton Junior School, Ferryhill

HIGH FORCE

The water's flowing
The wind is blowing
It's really high
The water flows by
Plunging, plunging ever down
Making such a loud, loud sound
Rocks clashing round and round
Day and night
Never stopping
Always dropping.

Paul Smith (11)
Chilton Junior School, Ferryhill

THE HIGHWAYMAN'S REVENGE

'Twas the night before Christmas in the 1900s
And the clouds of dust surrounded the dark hollow
Waiting to slay him after he slew me
I'll jump out of the hollow and kill him
Then your heart will rot through the night.

Jonathon Hunt (9)
Chilton Junior School, Ferryhill

SILVER FISH

Once there was a silver fish
Who'd give you a fabulous wish
Maybe a palace of gold
A kingdom to behold
Or wisdom more than anyone can hold.

Sophie Eddy (9)
Chilton Junior School, Ferryhill

MY SISTER

My sister, my sister
She's a very twisty sister
She goes in a mood with me
But she's my sister

My sister, my sister
She never shuts up
She messes my room
But she's my sister

My sister, my sister
She gets me into trouble a lot
She eats all my sweets
But she's my sister

My sister, my sister
After I've read her a story
She normally goes to bed
Now that's my sister.

Rebecca Moody (8)
Chilton Junior School, Ferryhill

HALLOWE'EN

Cackling witches,
Pointing hats,
Creepy crawlies,
Prowling cats,
Big black rats
And flying bats,
Hallowe'en is here, hold on to your hats.

Daniel Bargewell (10)
Chilton Junior School, Ferryhill

MY SISTER

M y sister is nice and quiet
Y oungest in my family

S he likes running around the house
I think she is a wild animal
S he has lots of friends
T oo many friends I think she has
E veryone loves her
R unning fast around the room

M y sister is loud
Y oung and funny

S he likes cats and so do I
I think she's mad about cats
S he likes mice as well
T oo loud and funny
E veryone likes her
R unning slowly around the house.

Amy Parkinson (10)
Crook Primary School, Crook

MY BABY SISTER

My baby sister, she's a pain,
She takes my toys, she drives me insane,
She screams and screams all through the night,
The next morning she broke my kite.
She pulls my hair, she hides my slippers,
She even lost my brand new flippers.
She gets her way with Mum and Dad,
You have to say, she's really bad,

My baby sister, she's a pain,
She takes my clothes, she drives me insane,
She hurts my cat, she eats my sweets,
She also hit my dog with a plastic seat.
She tears pages out of my books,
She spits out food when I cook.
Well you have to say they are all like that,
But you have to know, mine's a rat.

Alexandra Brook (9)
Crook Primary School, Crook

UNTITLED

H   ate is a powerful word
A   nd will affect you more than anything
T   his word should never be used
E   nd of story!

L   ove is a thing that will make you cry
O   ver and over again
V   ery, very hard to explain
E   ndless feelings deep inside

P   assion is shared between two people in love
A   nd very romantic, I must say
S   ecrets deep inside
S   ecrets that will never die
I   nside of you, this feeling never shows
O   n and on, no one knows
N   ever ever let it go.

Stephen Amos (10)
Crook Primary School, Crook

WATERFALLS

W ater flowing like a jacuzzi in the rocks
A ngel Falls feels like you are sleeping on a beach in South
America where it lives
T umbling somersaulting down the rocky cliff
E very sound it makes, sounds like flying through the
fluffy white clouds
R uffling through the rocks see how the water
F illing the rainforest with billions of waves of joy
A ll over the world there are waterfalls
L oudly crushing down the 300 foot cliff
L iking to sing and crash down the rocks
S ometimes it tempts people to swim in the bubbly water that gleams.

Emily Hull (9)
Crook Primary School, Crook

AUSTRALIA

A ustralia gets hotter and hotter until it's scorching hot
U sually you boil to a crisp, I should know I went there
S lithering and slouching, you are so hot
T elling tales of the cold place you live
R iding the car with the window shut and the air conditioning on
so you don't get hot
A lizard slithers along the floor
L ike he's never come to cold before
I went to Australia for my holiday
A nd it took a long time to get there.

Vivienne Robson (10)
Crook Primary School, Crook

ANIMAL

A   is for an animal that will not bite,
N   is for a nagging animal that will not bite,
I   is for inhabitant in the wild,
M   is for a mammal that is cowardly,
A   is for an ape called Alice,
L   is for an angry leopard,
S   is for a snake slithering around.

I   is for ill-mannered animals in the wild,
N   is for a newt that slithers in the water.

T   is for a tiger in the jungle,
H   is for a hippo in the murky, boiling, gooey mud,
E   is for an eagle hunting.

W   is for a whale in the glimmering water,
I   is for I want to save endangered animals in the wild,
L   is for looking after animals,
D   is for a dolphin curving in the sun.

Emma Jane Nelson (10)
Crook Primary School, Crook

MONDAY

M   onday is a terrible day
O   ne or two fights
N   obody hurt but they got wrong
D   irty and messy everybody was
A   nd today it was a terrible day because
Y   ou got wrong!

Jessica Berriman (10)
Crook Primary School, Crook

My Family

My family is the most precious thing to me,
They cook my tea,
My family look after me when I am not very well,
My brother always tells on me as well,
They get medicine for me when I've got the flu,
They look after me too.

My family makes me go to school,
So I don't act like a fool,
I like my mum,
She's very fun,
I like my dad,
But he gets mad,
I like my brother,
But he likes my mother.

Jade Burton (10)
Crook Primary School, Crook

The City Streets

The city streets are dull,
Robbers roam the streets,
Mugging you for everything you have got.

When you are in the city,
Why don't you look up and see buildings,
Larger than life.

That is what is on the street,
Muggers, buildings, all different shapes and sizes,
But remember you will only see these on city streets!

Michael Hughes (9)
Crook Primary School, Crook

SNOW

Snow time is cold,
Snowflakes fall onto the ground
From up in the clouds that look like fluffy bushes,
There is lots of snow on the ground.

The snowflakes become fainter and fainter,
Then the snow won't lie on the ground,
Even though it is extremely exciting,
The snow slowly disappears.

Before that, children play all day in the snow
And are making snowmen,
But shortly after that,
The snow has all gone.

Kirsty Chatterton (9)
Crook Primary School, Crook

THE NIGHT SKY

I stare up into the inky sky
And what do you think meets my eye?
Thousands of stars floating up there,
Like little diamonds glittering in the air.
The moon shines light to the Earth below,
Showering us with a huge yellow glow.
An aeroplane soars overhead,
With its lights shining so it can see ahead.
Everything up there fascinates me,
There are hundreds of things you can see.
Such as the clouds that are coming, which are midnight-black,
Which sneak closer and won't go back.

Emma Toogood (10)
Crook Primary School, Crook

IN SPACE

Travelling in space
In that very big place,
You're flying around
Off the ground in space.

Staring at the stars,
Going to land on Mars,
Flying away
But you want to stay in space.

Cruising the Milky Way
But only for a day
I'm on my way to Neptune
And my journey ends at the moon in space.

Jenna Weir (9)
Crook Primary School, Crook

SUMMERTIME

S   ummer is a happy time
U   nder the trees some people lie
M   um is pegging out the clothes
M   any people are having fun
E   veryone is very happy
R   eally hot everywhere
T   oday we play on our bikes
I   n-between everyone
M   e and my friends are very happy
E   veryone is enjoying summer.

Sam Green (9)
Crook Primary School, Crook

THE STRANGE PLANET

The planet is a sphere
Everyone is different
They can see and hear
They live in a tent
And it's all loud and clear

The aliens are red
They have funny snouts
Half of them are dead
They like eating trout
And the leader's called Fred

They don't like curry
Because it is hot
They are always in a hurry
They'd rather have a pot of money.

Jonathon Plumb (9)
Crook Primary School, Crook

MY LITTLE SISTER

My little sister beams,
But sometimes she screams.
My little sister cries,
But when I say a lullaby
She goes to sleep.
My little sister has a big bum,
But she always pinches my bubblegum.
My little sister has blonde hair,
She always pinches my teddy bear.
My little sister gets on my nerves
And always pinches Mum's best herbs.

Holly Clark (9)
Crook Primary School, Crook

FANTASTIC FOOTBALL

Charging down the wing,
With the ball at your feet,
Past two defenders,
Now the keeper is beat.

The ball is in the net,
You go to celebrate,
Now back into start positions,
You've got to concentrate.

The opponents draw one back,
Oh it is so tragic,
The visitors fans go wild,
They think it's a piece of magic.

You knock it past a defender,
With a silky flick,
Another pushes you over,
It is a *penalty kick*.

You give it a mighty whack,
It's a bit of a spinner,
It hits the back of the net,
This could be the winner.

The final whistle blows,
Everybody cheers,
The captain runs over
And says, 'I'll buy the beers.'

Kyle Johns (11)
Dene House Primary School, Peterlee

SUDDEN DEATH

As we dive into the sea,
Oh look, I can see,
The old ship wrecked in the storm,
The broken timber is the norm,
Dive further down, colder and colder,
The ship starts to look older and older,
Something shiny catches my eye, so bold,
Under the timber lies some gold,
Quickly hide, great white shark,
Lurking beneath in the dark!
Will I get out alive?
Will I ever get out alive?
My oxygen runs out,
I tried to shout!
I can see the white light,
Big, beautiful and bright!

Tom Ward (11)
Dene House Primary School, Peterlee

THE BEACH

Children splashing in the deep blue sea,
Fishermen catching fishes for their tea.
The sun is shining bright,
The wind is holding their kites.
Golden sand glistens so bright,
It makes the beach feel just right!
These are all the things that being by the sea,
Really means to me!

Mariel Jones (10)
Dene House Primary School, Peterlee

HIDDEN TREASURE

The pirates found the treasure
And shared it out with pleasure.
The captain got the most,
Then they all had a toast.

One was very sly,
He put a little by,
But the captain saw him
Out of the corner of his eye.

The enemy pirates attacked,
One of the boats got cracked.
The cannons got shot in the air,
But the pirates didn't care.

The pirates with the treasure won
And went to the pub for some fun.

Daryl Wheatley (10)
Dene House Primary School, Peterlee

THE LETTER

I wrote myself a poem,
A love letter actually,
I told myself that I was great
And I was meant to be.

This letter did continue,
It went on for a while,
I told myself I was the best
And I had super style.

My mother hasn't seen it,
Neither have my friends,
I think I'll keep it safe with me,
Until this weird craze ends.

Amy Mercer (11)
Dene House Primary School, Peterlee

MATCH DAY

As I walk down the bridge to the stadium,
I hear the crowd roar,
My ears go numb,
I go through the turnstile door.
I get a drink of lemonade,
Walking up the ramp to my seat,
The music fades,
Out come the lads.
Kick-off has passed half an hour ago,
No real atmosphere,
Until Sunderland go up and score,
There is a big cheer!
Half-time has just passed,
Not a good scoreline,
Only a draw,
We have half an hour to break the deadline,
The lads are tired,
There is no sign
Of a goal,
Until Phillips is clean through,
What a beautiful goal!

Jonathan Smith (11)
Dene House Primary School, Peterlee

NEIGHBOURS

A cowgirl lives in my town,
She lives next to the boy with the crown.
They live opposite a right pair of snobs,
But I have to say they have really good jobs.
Down the street are a right friendly pair,
They're so friendly, they're really rare,
Now the people who live over the road,
They always seem to use Morse code.
Next the people who live next door, they're nice
And they have pet mice
Named Tilly and Bendy
And a daughter called Wendy.
That brings me to the end of my town,
I hope you don't leave me with a frown.

Demitra Catleugh (11)
Dene House Primary School, Peterlee

MY BROTHER AND SISTER

My baby brother is so cute,
He is only a baby and he smiles a lot.
I love to hold him in my arms,
I just love him lots and lots.
He is very ticklish,
My little brother Lewis.

My little sister is very cute,
She likes to play with me.
She loves to watch the Tweenies
And always plays with Barbie dolls,
She likes to play outside,
My little sister Katie.

Aimee Beth Williams (10)
Dene House Primary School, Peterlee

MY HOT AIR BALLOON

Red, blue, green, yellow, the hot air balloon I dream of,
We start off at dawn, the adventure begins,
The scenery's breathless down below,
I wonder where we could go,
Maybe Africa where the lions roar
Or where busy people are.
Spain, the dancers dance in the hot sun,
The hot air balloon I dream of,
Leaving your troubles behind,
I wonder where we could go,
Maybe somewhere hot or
Maybe where there's snow.
Horrible landing, oh no you could fall!
My dream of my hot air balloon.

Caitlin Bell (11)
Dene House Primary School, Peterlee

TWILIGHT TIME

As the moon arose in the east,
Howling came from the forest beast,
Horses' shadows ran across the plain,
All the colours of twilight.

Whistling winds blew through naked trees,
Whispering, whistling, gentle breeze,
Animals came out to see the sight
Of beautiful, beautiful *twilight.*

Laura Greener (10)
Dene House Primary School, Peterlee

FOREST FRIGHT

In the forest, it was plain to see,
So many eyes were watching me.
Creatures scuttling here and there,
Which gave me quite a little scare.
I took a deep breath, said my prayers,
As lions approached me from their lairs.
I ran and hid behind a tree,
With all the eyes still watching me.
A deer stood proud, beneath the moon,
Batting its chest stood a hairy baboon.
Tiger's eyes, glowing so bright,
Fear upon me, I clenched my fists tight.
Its teeth are sharp, it likes your taste,
You body better move - post haste.
You better run, you better hide,
You're tiger's prey, you feel inside.
A colony of ants sprout from the ground,
Crickets were clicking, making a cracking sound.
Silken webs are glistening in the moonlight,
Stars are shining brightly in the dark night.
The sound of wolves makes me shiver
And the sound of howling made me quiver.
I was as stiff as a statute standing alone,
'Oh, I wish I was warm, all snug at home.'
I tried to find my way home with concentration,
Then I reached my destination.
As I walked out of the forest it was plain to see,
So many eyes were watching me.

Leah Allan (11)
Dene House Primary School, Peterlee

UNDER THE SEA

Under the sea where the Titanic lies
And where the dolphins swim,
Where the treasure sleeps,
Like badgers in the night,
Some fish are gold or maybe silver,
That's my idea of under the sea.

Under the sea where the shark stalks,
The beautiful yellow fish,
The chase is on, the shark attacks,
The fish are on the run
Like Linford Christie,
Running the hundred metre race,
That's my idea of under the sea.

Matthew Field
Dene House Primary School, Peterlee

THE SEASICK SERPENT

There was a seasick serpent,
Who lived in the Irish Sea,
He fed on all the things he found,
Including my friends and me.

He hasn't even caught us yet,
But I'm sure he will one day,
We'll have to make a plan to escape,
There's got to be a way.

His belly started to rumble,
As the sea storm began,
His face had turned a sickly green,
He looked awful - so we ran!

Rachel Ward (10)
Dene House Primary School, Peterlee

WHAT ARE FEELINGS?

W hat are feelings?
H ave we all got feelings?
A re they all sad feelings?
T he feelings that are good, enjoy them all.

A horrible feeling is like being called a name,
R eading all about feelings,
E njoy *your* feelings!

F riends *never* hurt our feelings!
E ars listen to other people's feelings.
E xpression changes when it's my turn!
L ying awake at night, thinking about my feelings.
I try to forget about my bad feelings.
N ever liked my feelings anyway!
G oing to make my feelings happier!
S o, what are feelings?

Jodie Lee Forster (10)
Dene House Primary School, Peterlee

WHEATUS (A SINGER)

W is for the best singer in the world,
H e is handsome, that's what he is,
E is for an excellent singer - he is,
A is for 'A Little Respect', the best song in the world,
T is for lots of trouble, I would make to see him,
U is for unusual songs he sings, but I still love him,
S is for super love, I would give to him.

Beckie Legg (11)
Dene House Primary School, Peterlee

WINTER FOREST AND SUMMER SUN

In the heart of the forest,
Where the snow lies white as sheep,
Trees lay bare, nothing to hide the forest creatures,
Under the leaves, the hedgehogs lie sleeping,
In the earth, moles are digging,
The moon is shining upon the crystallised snow,
Now it is winter, there is nowhere to go!

Animals come out of hibernation,
Now it's summer all over the nation.
All the creatures have come out,
All the children are playing about.
Now it's summer all over again,
I hope the summer never ends.

Jamie Maitland (11)
Dene House Primary School, Peterlee

MY CUDDLY DOG

M y dog Mac is very cute,
Y elling for a biscuit.

C alling when he needs a walk,
U sually he is very good,
D odging in and out of chairs,
D iving to see me when I come in,
L ively, playing with his toys,
Y elling if I hurt him.

D iving in a river,
O nly quiet when he is asleep,
G etting very hungry, he runs to the cupboard,
   My dog Mac.

Emma Hilton (10)
Dene House Primary School, Peterlee

MY CAT MINNIE

Fluff and fur,
Friendly purr,
Sleeps all day,
Then goes out to play.
Out all night,
Black and white,
When she's bad,
She acts quite mad,
When she's sweet,
She gets treats to eat.
Naughty but nice,
Catches mice,
Fat not skinny,
My cat Minnie!

Kimberley Russell (11)
Dene House Primary School, Peterlee

NIGHT-TIME

Darkness falls,
An owl calls,
The moon shines,
A clock chimes
And people sleep,
Without a peep.
But now night is behind
And morning unwinds,
The light is here
And darkness withers,
But again the night comes,
Darkness has won.

Matthew Pugh (10)
Dene House Primary School, Peterlee

SEASONS

Springtime is here, flowers bloom,
Blossom appears on the trees.
Rabbits running all day long,
Is this your favourite time of year?

It's summertime again at the beach,
Football, beach ball, many games to play,
Children playing by the sea,
Parents sunbathing in the summer sun.

Autumn is here, leaves are falling off the trees,
Red, brown, yellow, all colours of the rainbow,
Animals go into hibernation,
Winter is just around the corner.

Snowflakes are falling upon the crystallised snow,
Cars are covered with snow, like moving snowmobiles,
Snowmen are dancing in the moonlight,
Can you cope with the cold, crisp air?

Antony Price (11)
Dene House Primary School, Peterlee

LEGS

Legs of the giraffe are so slender,
Legs of the ladybird are quite tender.
Legs of the dinosaur are so strong,
Legs of a skunk really pong!
Legs of a tortoise are so old,
I wouldn't swap my legs for a large bag of gold.

Liam Harper
Dene House Primary School, Peterlee

THE FIRE IN THE HOUSE

The fire waving at the bottom of the chimney
As you step in this great big house
Everybody can feel the warmth inside
As the morning light shines in, it is freezing cold in the room
As the cold wind strides through

The clear wide window
So you can see the rain outside
The fire is nearly dead
But then the coal jumps in and it comes back to life again
The light shines on the golden daffodils when they are looking down
The picture that is on the wall is looking at me
I believe that they are very alive.

Sandy Lung (11)
Elleray Preparatory School, Windermere

THE GRAND ROOM

As I watch the time go by
I focus on the tick-tock
The floor, a railway track
Never-ending, as it seems
But out of the murk, a colour of rest
The walls so clear inside the house
Yet the cold still chills your heart

I contemplate the smell of reluctant peace
The chime, then cuckoo of the hour
The wood of the age
A face squared on the wall
He stands so great and strong
No cares for the goings on
His time grows, then it dies.

Alexander Farthing (10)
Elleray Preparatory School, Windermere

DOVE COTTAGE

In the warmest room in the house, all is calm.
As the fire roars and crackles, I hear the faint cuckoo
as another hour passes.
The dark gloom from the walls makes the room cosy,
as we settle from the cold winds outside.

Into the kitchen, growling like a lion, the warm fire glows.
Smells of smoke and roasting meat pass through me
as if it were really here.
Shadows form when ghost-like figures float past.

Tick-tock goes the tall, stick-like figure of the grandfather clock.
Walls like Turkish delight and a box full of memories
sitting on the side of the wall.

Here is a house filled with poetry, each waking day two centuries ago.
The laureate still looks down on us
and every person who enters that house.

Laurie Raymond (10)
Elleray Preparatory School, Windermere

THE KITCHEN

The blazing fire lashes out its warmth to fill the room with heat,
Wandering rats scurry onto the freezing floor,
The cooking pot whistles like a joyful child,
The candles burn their essence of light,
The rocking chair sways as the gentle breeze passes through,
The slates form an endless path of mystery and stories to tell,
The lonely rug sits quietly waiting for its addicted owner.

Barnaby Martin (10)
Elleray Preparatory School, Windermere

THE CUCKOO CLOCK

As I stand beneath the clock,
The painting on the wall,
I get a sudden feeling that I am being watched.

As the clock ticks I get a sudden shiver,
Running down my spine,
Trying to tempt me to the blazing fireplace.

The clock ticks as the hours go by,
This truly is a mechanical mystery,
As the golden pendulum tries to hypnotise,
Like a clock on a chain.

As the clock stands up straight,
It acts like a strong man,
Like a soldier in battle.

Andrew Harvey (11)
Elleray Preparatory School, Windermere

THE KITCHEN

The hanging meat is nearly brown
And almost ready to cook,
The cupboard full of flour and herbs,
Rosemary hangs from high above,
Scenting the kitchen air.

The stones lie cold while the kettle boils,
The room is dancing while the flames lap against the bars,
Coal is poured onto the dying embers,
The flames spring back to life
And light up the once darkened room.

Harry Wilson (11)
Elleray Preparatory School, Windermere

HUNGRY FIRE

It sits there black as night,
Bearing no warmth, nor light,
Waiting to be lit, by its creator,
Wearing its black patterned armour,
Shining gently in the window light,
It smells its food,
Hot and steaming in a bucket,
It eats its food with great delight,
The flames rapidly grow higher,
Flying higher the red sparks glow,
In the middle a fiery battle,
Roaring, raging,
Evermore till it dies away.

Tristan Tinn
Elleray Preparatory School, Windermere

LIFE

I'm fed up with homework and maths
Same with the cleaning and baths
My mum always tells me to tidy my room
And chases me around with the end of her broom
I wish I was wild and free
And didn't have veg for my tea
Jobs and chores that's what I hate
Watching TV, that will be great
'Comb your hair!'
It's just not fair.

Sam Mallard (10)
Gosforth CE Primary School, Seascale

GYMNASTICS

Forward flip
Legs split
Handstand
On the ground
Forward roll
Like a ball
Carting about
On the rope
Swinging round
Aching hands
Twist down
To the ground
Fall down
Into bridge
Jump up
Final position
Handstand
Hot and tired
Tight clothes
Stand straight
Take a bow.

Joanne Buchanan (11)
Gosforth CE Primary School, Seascale

IF

If my mum was an animal
She would be a monkey
Cheeky but loveable
Swinging swiftly to me for a cuddle

If my mum was a flower
She would be a rose
Strong but spiky
With red, warm petals

If my mum was a colour
She would be yellow
Sweet yellow
Bright and breezy

If my mum was an instrument
She would be a tuba
Low-pitch, big and soft
Sometimes with an odd squeak.

Becky Paul (9)
Gosforth CE Primary School, Seascale

TRAIN

Faster than horses, faster than bulls
View changes as the train pulls
Passing the mountains
Squirting fountains
Chugging along, all is calm
Here comes a shower
The train makes power
Cars whizz past
Train going fast
Keeps on track
Clickety clack
Swishes and sway
The train makes its way
Nearly there
All is fair
At last we're there.

Joanne Buchanan, Rachel Flynn & Rebecca Simpson (10)
Gosforth CE Primary School, Seascale

HELICOPTER

Speeding through the clear blue sky,
Faster than the blink of an eye.
People building massive flats,
The bins are swarming with stray cats.
Factories belching out grey smoke,
Football hooligans fighting folk.
Bridges and walls graffiti-sprayed,
From our aerial view all is displayed.

Jack Denwood (10)
Gosforth CE Primary School, Seascale

CHILDREN OF THE WEEK

Monday's child is short and stroppy
Tuesday's child is big and bossy
Wednesday's child is silly and smelly
Thursday's child pours custard in his welly
Friday's child is a good little boy
Saturday's child loves the Wild West
Sunday's child is the best of the best!

Ben Pearce (10)
Gosforth CE Primary School, Seascale

DIESEL TRAIN

One hundred and twenty miles per hour
Going through tunnels by the hour
Outside, factories belching out smoke
People on streets like ordinary folk

Speeding past huge suspension bridges
Carefully going along dangerous ridges
Silently we glide through the night
We wake up to the sun's morning light.

Liam O'Donnell (11)
Gosforth CE Primary School, Seascale

ELECTRIC TRAIN

Faster than Porsches, faster than Snitches
Fields and meadows, birds and ditches
Speeding along like horses that race
Robbers that run that police cannot trace
All of the buildings and passing trains
Flying through the acid rains
Sadly again in the wink of an eye
 Polluted cities whistle by.

Owain Pugh, Craig Naylor & Stuart Kirby (10)
Gosforth CE Primary School, Seascale

CHILDREN OF THE WEEK

Monday's child is hardworking and quick,
Tuesday's child is never ever sick,
Wednesday's child is beautiful and sweet,
Thursday's child is ever so neat,
Friday's child is good as gold,
Saturday's child is bright and sweet,
Sunday's child has lovely smelling feet.

Claire Crayston (11)
Gosforth CE Primary School, Seascale

THE FIELD TRIP

This day I went down to the beach,
The tide was rolling out of sight,
When the sun shone down,
The water looked like shaken tin foil.

White horses galloped out at sea,
Seagulls stood in line, like sergeants,
Dogs ran over the sand,
Fast like the wind, tails wagging.

Sinking sand sucked your boots in,
Strange dinosaur feet,
Writing in the sand
With a Wellington pen.

Stones and shells like ornaments,
One shaped like a bone,
My hair as wavy as the sea,
In my eyes.

This day I went down to the beach,
On a trip with Mrs Field,
What an adventure!

Isla Frost-Pennington (9)
Harecroft Hall School, Seascale

ROBOT WARS

Dim the lights, cue the applause
Now it's time for Robot Wars
3, 2, 1, activate!

See it flip through the air
Metal flying everywhere
Flip! Bang! Smash!
Is it Matilda or Sergeant Bash?

Look at all the metal
Could it be dead or alive?
Down goes the pit,
Cease!

Rickie Bewsher (9)
Harecroft Hall School, Seascale

WATERY ZOO

I am Cancer the crab
I belong on the beach
Hiding out amongst rocks
And out of the reach
Of seagulls and puffins
For I am their prey
This is my home
Safely hidden away
I am friends with the lobster
Cousins are we
In our watery world
Deep under the sea
Mermaids and swordfish
Rainbowfish too
Live here in the blue
Of our watery zoo
Sand worms and pelicans
Octopus and squid
We have to be careful
As they are quite big!
Dolphins and sealions
From the great to the small
Whether lovely or ugly
The sea loves them all!

Joanna Bentley (8)
Harecroft Hall School, Seascale

MY MUMMY!

I will always remember the lovely soft touch
The cuddly touch I love so much
The person that will forever be bubbly
Ah, a loving smile, how pretty
The yummy taste that is creamy and sweet
Always tidying, so it's so neat

The adult that makes you smile
Makes you angry, but only for a while
Being apart, that makes me cry
My friends are caring but only for a sigh
She is very pretty
Caring too
Always a place in her heart for you

Bet you can't guess who I mean
The person who is always on the scene
One person who makes it sunny
Yes
Your very own mummy!

Kathryn Mrowicki (11)
Harecroft Hall School, Seascale

SCHOOL DINNER

I'll never forget the bell at 12:30,
For I knew it was time to get dirty,
We are now lining up in the dinner line,
Whoever serves this is committing a crime!

If you like it you must be mad,
For this food is really bad,
As I roll up my sleeves,
You can hear the screams.

Food fight!
It really is a terrific sight,
That is what makes dinner so fun,
Well, it cheers the teacher up for one!

Becky Holliday (11)
Harecroft Hall School, Seascale

THE ICE CREAM SONG

Do you like ice cream?
I do, I do!
The small, the big, the medium too
Do you like ice cream?
I do, I do!
The sticky, the chewy, the creamy too
Why do you like ice cream?
O why? O why?
Its shape, its size, I wonder why
Why do you like ice cream?
O why? O why?
It gets on your clothes
It's sticky too and the way
It has an oozing stick of thick, creamy chocolate too
I like ice cream
Because, because
The taste, the smell, the texture too
And the crispy wafer, the big fat cherry and
Last of all, its flavouring is smelly
That's why, that's why
I like ice cream
That's why, that's why, that's why!

Rosanna Ponticelli (10)
Harecroft Hall School, Seascale

GETTING UP!

I hate getting up in the morning
With all the poking and prodding
Why can't I stay in bed?
Please let me be
I really want to sleep
Can't I stay in bed
And tuck up with my bear
Who's really sweet and blue?
Please let me stay in bed
And rest my little head
I hate getting up in the morning.

Dhriti Eapen (10)
Harecroft Hall School, Seascale

FIRE

The sun is shining
The birds are singing
On a Monday
Two boys are playing with matches
They let go
And in a blow a fire erupted
Like a volcano
Everyone is getting baked.

Thomas Gleave (11)
Harecroft Hall School, Seascale

CATS

Cats
Small, thin and fat,
The lightning flash,
As quick as they dash

They jump and pounce,
For mice that weigh an ounce,
The birds fly high,
That walk and then die.

Rebecca Morris-Eyton (10)
Harecroft Hall School, Seascale

MY GARDEN

I have a garden,
Flowers grow,
My favourite are the roses,
We have red roses
And yellow ones too,
They smell fabulous,
Especially in the summer,
That is when we sit on our bench
And watch the water of our fountain,
Glistening in the sun.

Tasha Bradley (10)
Harecroft Hall School, Seascale

WHEN I GET UP

When I get up, I jump out of bed
Then I race downstairs
I brush my teeth for two minutes
Then I slap some soap on my cloth
To my face and . . .
Rub, rub, rub, I'm clean now
Then I'm off again, racing back to my room.

Marcus Brough (10)
Harecroft Hall School, Seascale

MY DREAM

I dreamt I was a starfish
In the middle of the sea
With seagulls flying up above
And parrotfish surrounding me

A piece of clay sailed past
From a wreck on the sea floor
I dived down deep below the wave
I wanted to know more

I wanted to see what I looked like
In a silver spoon found on the wreck
I saw a star-shaped lump of sugar
Bobbing around on the deck

I then heard a noise in the background
Waaahh! Came a cry in the night
I woke up and the dream was all over
Back to my boring old life!

Alistair Mackintosh (8)
Harecroft Hall School, Seascale

CASTLES

A grey shadow upon the night,
Standing still without any light,
Battles litter the land like scars,
Blood, death and night block out any light,
Kings come out to fight,
Killing all the knights,
Shadows creep out into the daylight,
Then the next night there is no life.

Fraser Frost-Pennington (10)
Harecroft Hall School, Seascale

THE SEA

I was on the sea one day,
While the crashing wind whistled away,
The shells of blue, the many hues,
Like the sky.

Pebbles look like small round balls,
The waves echoed the seagulls call,
White horses jumped high.

Wet sand was like coffee cake,
Rock pools made a baby lake,
With cockle shells.

Emma Moore (9)
Harecroft Hall School, Seascale

TREASURE HUNT

Waves roar and crash on the sand,
Water foams, swirling round my hand,
Shells smooth against my skin.

Seagulls screech as they fly,
Children's voices fill the sky,
Sand, gritty between my fingers.

Stones polished, shine like tin,
Rocks like loaves of bread,
Wade in up to your knees
And dig for sunken treasure.

Patrick Morris-Eyton (8)
Harecroft Hall School, Seascale

THE TIGER

He silently slips through the long grass,
His eyes like diamonds or rubies red,
A low growl creeps from his jaws,
On the grass he wipes the blood from his claws,
He pauses a second, crouching low,
So heavily built, that muscular figure,
There's a glimpse of a deer,
His slow run becomes a sprint,
So speedy, he leaves no print,
The coat of orange and black,
He leaps on the animal's back,
Slits the windpipe with one swipe,
The beast takes his fill,
He strolls steadily back,
Back to his family in the lair.

Laurence Gribble (10)
Harecroft Hall School, Seascale

CHOCOLATE

Chocolate is delicious, especially when it's melting,
It's sweet, sticky and runny too,
It can be square, rectangular or even triangular
And crunchy when you chew.

Chocolate has fantastic sweet smells,
With a colour of thick brown or white,
It can be rich and sickly, but it always goes quickly,
So why don't you just take a bite?

Elspeth Block (10)
Harecroft Hall School, Seascale

THE SNAKE

Slowly the hungry snake creeps upon its prey
It slithers over the ground towards the unsuspecting rat
The snake hisses in hunger as it slowly opens its mouth
Venom drips from the snake's huge, sharp fangs
The blood from its last kill still remains on them
The snake edges closer and closer
It raises its head and prepares to kill
Before the rat can think, the snake turns upon him with no mercy
The rat is fighting well
But it is no match for the mighty serpent
After a hard battle the rat is dead
And the snake is hungry no longer.

James Cater (11)
Harecroft Hall School, Seascale

THE WIND

Oh, the wind blows in your ear,
Sometimes so fast you cannot hear.
The wind blows in the trees
And the leaves fall down,
Which make people frown.
In autumn the trees are bare
Thanks to the wind!
It makes leaves twirl, whirl and swirl
In a lovely pattern in the air,
Sometimes wind is good for you don't have to care,
The wind is usually bad which is not at all rare.

Rebecca Anderson (10)
Hartside Primary School, Crook

WHAT'S HIDING IN MY HOUSE?

Monsters in my house,
Got in through the window,
Make me feel so scared,
Voices all around me,
Could there be a ghost in my bedroom cabinet?
I'm sure I have just seen one swimming in the toilet,
A cyclops in the kitchen and a bogeyman under the stairs,
You'll never guess what it is -
My brother trying to scare us!

Thomas Craggs (10)
Hartside Primary School, Crook

SHARKS

Sharks are big and strong
And swim in the sea all day long.
They eat fish with their big, spiky teeth,
Sometimes they catch a thief
In a blown-up boat and the sharks have him for tea,
Sometimes they want more
And go to the shore.

Anthony Conley (9)
Hartside Primary School, Crook

THE FOUR SEASONS

Spring, summer, autumn and winter
The four seasons of the year
Flowers, beaches, leaves and snow, brings happiness or woe
Flowers are beautiful, the beach is hot
Leaves are untidy when they start to rot.

Liam Bailey (9)
Hartside Primary School, Crook

MY FAMILY

My mum is a dark-haired woman who cooks and cleans,
All day long my mum dries the clothes as the sun beams.
My brother has lots of friends and Action Men,
For Christmas he bought me a new pen.
My dad is reading a new thriller book,
He, like my mum, is a good cook.
My gran is on the ladies' darts team
And loves to watch football on the TV screen.

Jordan Paige Gent (10)
Hartside Primary School, Crook

UNDER MY BED

I don't know what's under my bed,
'Hello, who's there?' I say.
'It is I, the hairy, scary bear, I've been under here all day.
I want to suck your blood and crunch your bones, till they go mush.
Then I'll take out both your eyeballs and turn them into slush.'
'But Mr Monster, Sir, how should I go to the loo?'
'I'm sorry to say you can't or I'll eat you.'

Laura Hook (10)
Hartside Primary School, Crook

GOLDEN TREASURE

Looking for treasure down at the bottom of the sea,
Where can it be?
People go down to the bottom of the sea,
Looking for it and there it is in a dark lonely corner,
They go up to it and open it, what can it be?
Staring down at us, some gold *treasure!*

Helen Hodges (10)
Hartside Primary School, Crook

THE SNOW

Once there was a bit of snow,
It started to glow,
It was freezing cold
And it was big and bold,
It is like a crime,
Winter's freezing all the time,
It freezes your face,
Wear warm clothes just in case.

Michael Winter (9)
Hartside Primary School, Crook

MY MUM

My mum is kind,
My mum is cool,
She doesn't make me clean my room.
When I am feeling down,
She always takes away my frown.
I love my mum, she is so sweet,
She is like a golden treat.

Jessica Moore (10)
Hartside Primary School, Crook

A CREATURE IN MY BED

The creature in my bed
Has a big fat head,
He has a friend called Ted.
Who has a bump on his head.
He is fast asleep in my bed
With a bandage on his head.

Eamon Richardson (9)
Hartside Primary School, Crook

MY DOG

When I stand in front of my dog,
She licks my hand and sighs
And when I walk away from her,
She sits down and cries.
I throw her a bone,
When I'm all alone
And then it makes her happy.
I like her and she likes me,
I love my dog.

Laura Winter (9)
Hartside Primary School, Crook

MONSTERS

There's monsters in my bedroom
And some inside my bed,
Monsters hiding on the stairs
And monsters in my head.
They're everywhere I go
And everything I see,
Please, please monsters,
Will you leave me?

Emma Louise Colling (10)
Hartside Primary School, Crook

SILVER SNOW

Snow glows and sparkles in the night,
When I wake up, I see it glittering bright,
When I pick it up, it's like a ball of silver light,
The sun comes up to give us light.

Sarah Elizabeth Clarey (9)
Hartside Primary School, Crook

THE CAT

A small cat,
Chased a bat
And a fat rat,
That looked like Postman Pat.
Said, 'I tought I taw a puddy cat.'
The small cat was very fat
And could not run as fast as the bat.
So he chased the fat rat,
That looked like Postman Pat,
Instead of the fast bat!

Paul Harvey (9)
Hartside Primary School, Crook

MONSTERS

There's monsters in my cupboard,
There's monsters in my bed,
There's monsters in my teddy bears,
I don't think they've been fed.
Are they living or are they dead?
I don't know, they're talking in my head.

Sammie Lee Johnson (10)
Hartside Primary School, Crook

SNOW

The snow is like a frosty breeze,
If you stand in it, you will freeze.

If you play out in the snow,
It gives your cheeks a pinky glow.

Jonathan Mason (10)
Hartside Primary School, Crook

HIDDEN TREASURES

Deep down under the sea
Half a box I can see
Maybe it needs a key?
Here it is, under a rock
Opening it slowly
What a lot of treasure
Necklaces, rings, crystals too
Gems, diamonds
For me and you!

Linzi Nimmo (10)
Hensingham Junior School, Whitehaven

HIDDEN TREASURES

Gardens can be large
Gardens can be small
Flowers full of scent
Flowers in bloom
You could have your very own treasure
Just outside your own back door
Your garden can be your own treasure.

Emily Edgar (7)
Hensingham Junior School, Whitehaven

HIDDEN TREASURES

Here is treasure under the sea,
Nobody has found it except for me.
There is silver, gold and sparkly shells,
That is my treasure under the sea,
Hip, hip, hooray, it is amazing what you can see under the sea.

Heather Lewthwaite (7)
Hensingham Junior School, Whitehaven

HIDDEN TREASURES

Where could the treasure be?
Is it on planet Jupiter
Or planet Stupiter?

Where could the treasure be?
Maybe it could be under the sea
Or maybe it is quite near me?

Where could the treasure be?
Maybe it is right here
Or should I just give up and go and get a pint of beer?

Where could the treasure be?
Could it be buried under the ancient tree?
Yes! I think it could be.

I'll be rich, yes I will,
I am so excited, I can't stay still.

Where's my spade?
Here it is,
I wonder when the treasure was made?

James Linton (11)
Hensingham Junior School, Whitehaven

HIDDEN TREASURE

Down under the sea,
Over the twinkly stream,
Was a glass of golden tea,
But close by I had a lovely dream.

But then I found a box of toys,
Hidden under a holiday tree,
Then came up a group of boys,
They took all of my lovely toys away from me.

I thought that I had made some love,
With my wishes from the sky,
Then I sprayed some of my charming love,
That was all a silly lie.

Showers drifting from the sky,
Then I found something very high,
Why did that happen? I don't know why,
Then I said I could just cry.

Stephanie Lowrey (9)
Hensingham Junior School, Whitehaven

HIDDEN TREASURE

Down in the river,
Where nobody knows,
Four big chests of gold,
Lie in rows and rows.

They wait for years,
To be discovered or found,
I wonder who will be the lucky one
And end up rich with lots of pounds.

One day one chest
Began to float,
Only one girl had noticed it,
While rowing in a boat.

Now you've guessed
Who that girl could be,
No, not you or your friend,
Yes, of course it's *me*.

Maryam Umar (11)
Hensingham Junior School, Whitehaven

WHERE COULD THE HIDDEN TREASURE BE?

Where could the hidden treasure be?
Is it on the moon
Or is it on planet Zoom?

Where could the hidden treasure be?
Could it be where I think it could be
Or is it in the Mississippi?

Where could the hidden treasure be?
Could you tell me Mrs P
Or could you tell me Mr P?

Where could the hidden treasure be?
I only want the gold,
Even though it's stone cold.

Where could the hidden treasure be?
I know it's inside you,
No, it's inside me.

Daniel Tyson (11)
Hensingham Junior School, Whitehaven

HIDDEN TREASURE

Down in the deep dark sea,
Where the seaweed and sea urchins be,
There's a box half-hidden by sand and shells,
It has laid there for years and there it dwells,
No one knows what it holds,
But we know within it are jewels and gold,
So it will lie there forever and a day,
Or will someone find it?
Who can say!

Jade Rogan (10)
Hensingham Junior School, Whitehaven

HIDDEN TREASURE

Down, down at the bottom of the sea,
Too deep down for the eye to see.

There lays a chest which nobody knows,
It lays in front of rows and rows.

Even though it's not the only one there,
The person who finds it, I don't think will care.

There's something special about this chest,
If I could choose just one, it would be the best.

This treasure down at the bottom of the sea,
I know who will find it, not you, *me!*

Catherine Edgar (11)
Hensingham Junior School, Whitehaven

MY TREASURES

Down, down under the sea,
Is a chest full of gold,
Waiting for me,
So I'll dive down deep
To the bottom of the sea
And find the gold
Waiting for me
And when I find this chest of gold,
(I will look until I'm old,)
I will have millions of pounds,
I'll be the richest all around.

Samantha Cannings (9)
Hensingham Junior School, Whitehaven

BROOMSTICK GYMNASTICS

I look down
I see lots of tiny things
I see my house
A little speck of white and brown
Like dust on a green carpet
I feel wicked up in the air
I twist and turn about
Broomstick gymnastics!
Suddenly I go into a dive
I swoop towards the ground
My broomstick has broken down
Crash . . . down
             Down
                  Down.

Kayleigh Jones (8)
Heversham CE Primary School, Milnthorpe

THE WHITE SHEET

Cold, thick snow falling all about me
Smoothly
Lightly
Drifting
D
  O
    W
     N
Covering like a white sheet
Over the world's bed
Until boys came and ruined it
With their sledge.

Samuel Willacy (8)
Heversham CE Primary School, Milnthorpe

WHAT A LOT OF NOISE!

Zooming planes,
Children screaming,
Dogs barking,
Car exhausts smoking,
Chickens squawking,
Lamb baaing,
Cows mooing,
Squeaking wheels on cars,
Pigs oinking,
Ants nibbling,
Snakes slithering,
Horses galloping,
Rabbits sniffing,
What a lot of noise!

Emma Matthews (9)
Heversham CE Primary School, Milnthorpe

SNOW

Snowy hills covered with flakes
Like feathers shaken
Out of a pillow.
Soft white icing on a cake.
Snow gliding in the air.
Snow is like candyfloss at the fairground.
The snow tree.
The icy tree.
Ice drifting down.
Snowdrops covered with snow.
I shake the snow off the tree
Onto my brother, Jacob
And he cries, 'Snow, weeee.'

Jessica Rosser (8)
Heversham CE Primary School, Milnthorpe

MY BAD BOX

I will put in my box
the touch and the taste of evil

I will put in my box
the wicked red Devil
to stop him doing his stuff

I will put in my box
the snake's poison and the gorgon's glare

I will put in my box
the harsh noise of moose music

I will open my box
when people are horrid to me
and let them have a dose of their own medicine.

Thomas Davies (7)
Heversham CE Primary School, Milnthorpe

SCARY BOX

I will put in my box
A creepy spider that will go *booo*
A big, big crab and a shark that will kill
I will put in my box
A dog with sharp teeth
A devil with a red body that goes *roarrrr*
I shall let out of my box a scary dog
And remember it has very sharp teeth
Beware of my box!

Justine Walker (8)
Heversham CE Primary School, Milnthorpe

KEEPING HEALTHY

My nanna says . . . eat vegetables
I say chocolate bars, but she doesn't agree
She says eating crisps is OK

My nanna says . . . eat carrots
I say toast, but she doesn't agree
She says eating meat is OK

My nanna says . . . to eat chicken
I say sausages are best, but she doesn't agree
She says eating potato is OK

My nanna says . . . to go out to play
I say I like to watch the TV, but she doesn't agree
She says playing football is OK

This keeping healthy is difficult for Nanna
And me to agree!

Jack Smith (9)
Heversham CE Primary School, Milnthorpe

WATERFALL IN WINTER

Silver white-beaded curtains
  Glittering like stars
    Diamonds and pearls
      Sparkling in the dark night
        Crystal rocks crackle
          Shimmering in the moonlight.

Ashley Porter (8)
Heversham CE Primary School, Milnthorpe

MY JOURNEY THROUGH THE BODY

I went through the human body
I slid right down the throat
And in the rush of water
It was hard to keep afloat

I went into my stomach
It was slippery and slimy
I reached my sausagey intestines
All brown and grey and grimy

I climbed right up the body
Some speed I suddenly gained
Then I reached the cerebellum
And crawled into the brain

I saw some squirly, squiggly things
Like the tentacles of a giant squid
Now I can say I've journeyed inside
The body of a human kid.

Jonathan Hyman (7)
Heversham CE Primary School, Milnthorpe

DECAY IN THE GARDEN

Compost heaps make a whiff,
The bin reeks even more,
There's loads of rubbish
On the garden floor!

Rotting fungus on the grass,
Leaves are changing colour,
Mouldy apples on the floor,
My garden's getting duller!

My garden is a mess,
All because of decay,
I wish decay would . . .
Just go, go *away!*

Joanna Swinbank (10)
Heversham CE Primary School, Milnthorpe

I WONDER ABOUT RIVERS

The River Kent,
The River Thames,
Even the River Ouse,
All this water fame.

I wonder why it came?
I wonder where they flow to?
They might flow to the falls?
I wonder if there's bones in them?
I wonder if there's aqua halls?

The River Kent is long,
But not as long as some,
I wonder if the Amazon
Has a great grandmum.

The River Kent,
The River Thames,
Even the River Wye,
All this water fame,
I wonder why it came?

James Hyman (9)
Heversham CE Primary School, Milnthorpe

CAR TALK

Off we go to London!
Has everybody got their seatbelt on?
Yes Dad.
Are we nearly there yet?
No, not yet dear!
I spy with my little eye something beginning with S . . .
Are we nearly there yet?
No dear.
I spy with my little eye something beginning with A . . .
Mum, I feel sick!
Pick up your bucket dear.
Go to sleep.
I can't, I'm too excited!
Let's count lorries then.
1, 2, 3, 4 . . .
Are we nearly there?
No dear.
Have a sandwich.
OK, but when will we get there?
As soon as you stop asking!
OK, I've stopped asking, so . . .
Are we there yet?

Sophie Fishwick (7)
Heversham CE Primary School, Milnthorpe

HIGH ON THE MOUNTAIN

Chattering teeth like noisy drills,
Blasting blizzard freezing cold,
Mittens, scarf and winter jacket,
At the top there's thinner air,
High on the mountain.

With icy blasting snow,
Up on top, the eerie silence
And the cool whipping wind,
High above the clouds,
High on the mountain.

Jamie Keatings (11)
Heversham CE Primary School, Milnthorpe

DECAY

Leaves falling from the trees,
Jostling to the ground,
Slushy mud lying all around,
With a coating of crispy mess,
Crashing through the vegetation,
Going home for warmth.

Hedgehogs crawling through the hedge,
Ready for the hibernation,
Bugs are in the undergrowth,
Birds aren't in the trees,
Winter's coming back,
Crashing through the vegetation,
Going home again.

Rubbish lying on the compost heap,
Getting colder day by day,
Everything's rotting,
Winter is plotting,
Fungus growing,
Crashing through the vegetation,
Going home once more.

Liam Gannicliffe (11)
Heversham CE Primary School, Milnthorpe

THE SEA

At night when I'm in bed,
The sea gets angry and ferocious,
Roaring, screaming, spitting
Against my window.

Like a water volcano,
Erupting freezing water,
Crashing, thrashing, tearing
Against hard rocks.

Towering up and crashing down
On the sandy beach,
Bashing, punching, falling
Upon the sand.

I look out the next day
To see the innocent sea,
Lapping with now normal
Waves - calm.

Emily Crowder (9)
Heversham CE Primary School, Milnthorpe

CHILDREN SHOUTING

Outside, children shouting
Inside, children shouting
Down the road, children shouting
In the park, children shouting
In the school yard, children shouting
Everywhere, children shouting
What a lot of noise!

Max Shaw (9)
Heversham CE Primary School, Milnthorpe

MY PREHISTORIC BOX

I will put in my box
Deadly dinosaurs from
The Jurassic era
Beastly prehistoric bugs
The Stone Age flint axes

I will put in my box
The prehistoric people
From the Bronze Age
The remains of Iron Age buckets
The burial mounds from ancient times

I will make a present of the past
In my prehistoric box.

David Ely (8)
Heversham CE Primary School, Milnthorpe

WHAT A LOT OF TRAFFIC

The belching herd of cows,
The oinking group of pigs,
The barking pack of dogs,
The running coop of chickens,
What a lot of traffic.

The slamming doors of houses,
The squeaking wheels of cars,
The shouting children out playing,
The zooming planes in the sky,
What a lot of traffic.

Kirsty Tyson (9)
Heversham CE Primary School, Milnthorpe

MY A-Z OF KEEPING HEALTHY

Apples and bananas are supposed to be good to eat,
As are carrots and dates.
Eggs and fish give us all our protein,
Gravy and ham are fattening.
Ice lollies and jelly are not good for you,
Kiwi fruit and lemons are best to eat.
Milk and nectarines are recommended,
Oranges and pears are juicy.
Quavers and Rice Krispies are sometimes good,
Salad and tomatoes are the best,
Perhaps I should give up on the rest!

Emma Chapman (9)
Heversham CE Primary School, Milnthorpe

CLIMBING A MOUNTAIN

A steep rock face rising up high,
Eagles swooping from the sky,
The massive mountain in the wind,
Ascend to the freezing clouds,
Strong breeze on the icy mountain,
Jostling mist like a fountain,
The blizzard swishing surrounding the summit,
Blanking out my view below,
As I stand, I feel alone,
Except for the screeching birds' tone.

Nick Hamer (10)
Heversham CE Primary School, Milnthorpe

WATER WAR

Coming out of school, there is no need to quiver,
Because it's time for the fight in the river.

As we walk into battle,
All our hats start to rattle.
Here we go, we are starting the fight,
Our water guns are wobbling, so hold on tight.

Clashing, smashing, swirling water, flares of water rises,
Big splashes, small splashes, splashes of all shapes and sizes.

As we come to the end of our fight,
It's half-eight in the night.
We had to stop because of rain,
I hope we will play again.

Laurence Stannard (10)
Heversham CE Primary School, Milnthorpe

KEEPING HEALTHY!

Exercise, exercise
Blood flowing like a stream,
Attacking germs like a dream,
Exercise, exercise,
Blood cells hitting the sides,
Going down the body slides,
Exercise, exercise,
Jingling like tiny bells through my body,
That's my exercise.

Matty Cummins (10)
Heversham CE Primary School, Milnthorpe

RIVER KENT

I wonder where it starts?
In teeny tiny streams,
That will very slowly grow,
I wonder where it starts?

I wonder if it has a middle?
Probably in a giant river,
I know it will be slower,
I guess that that's its middle.

I wonder where it ends?
Probably in the sea.
I know, I'll race it there,
That's where I will be.

Douglas Parsons (9)
Heversham CE Primary School, Milnthorpe

SNOW

Giant coats on the trees
Lovely white, big leaves
Cold, cold
Everything cold
Everything cold on me
My nose is cold
My toes are cold
But that is how
It is meant to be.

Lauren Thompson (9)
Heversham CE Primary School, Milnthorpe

MY MAGIC BOX

I will put in my box
Stars from an open sky
A genie who will grant me
Everlasting wishes

A witch who will help me
Make potions

I will put in my box
A wand that glimmers and shines
In the night sky
A necklace that glitters
Like bright snow
With sparks flying out

I will open my box
When people are nice to me!

Laura Hamer (7)
Heversham CE Primary School, Milnthorpe

ICE

Crisp and frosty
Like white candyfloss
Hard and transparent
Like a window in the sea
It creaks and cracks
Crinkles and crackles
It's ice.

Paul Gibson (8)
Heversham CE Primary School, Milnthorpe

MEMORIES OF THE SUN

I am the sun,
Seeing the tiny pinheads of tall flats in the busy cities,
Seeing the green, green, scratchy bushes in the large fields,
Seeing the fluffy balls of plump sheep grazing contentedly.

I am the sun,
Tasting the hot fresh air swirling slowly around me,
Tasting the lovely happiness below.

I am the sun,
Smelling the smoky fires burning wispily,
Smelling the burnt barbeques of the laughing people below,
Smelling the fresh odour of the light rain.

I am the sun,
Feeling the light breeze blowing in my face, keeping me cool,
Feeling the warmth fingering me like a giant hand made of fire,
Feeling space stroking gently.

I am the sun,
Hearing the distant chatter below,
Hearing the cars cry like hungry babies,
Hearing the shutters go down on the final shop,
The silvery moon is rising and . . .
I am going . . .
Going . . .
Gone!

Bonnie Nicholson (8)
Lees Hill CE Primary School, Brampton

MEMORIES OF A TINY FISHING BOAT

It feels tiny fish with its keel as they dart by like fingertips tapping.
It feels the grains of sand hit the side of the boat like bullets from a gun.
It feels a dolphin thud against the side of the boat and then float
                                                    to the surface.

It sees huge ferries make enormous waves which break into
                                                    white horses.
It watches lifeboats speed away to rescue people whose lives
                                                    are in danger.
It sees people having fun on the beach, building sandcastles
                                                    and swimming.
It watches a lighthouse flash every so often, like an eye winking.

It hears the sea roar like a lion, as it comes rushing in to pounce
                                                    on the shore.
It hears the seagulls squealing as they peck up a chip or two.
It hears the high-pitched squeak of a dolphin in the distance.

It smells barbecued steaks from the coastal caravan site.
It smells the revolting smell of rotting fish being wafted over from
                                                    the fishing harbour.
It smells the salt in the air, which evaporated from the sea.
It smells the smoke from an old steamboat, giving rides to
                                                    mothers and children.

It tastes the nasty salt water, as the boat rocks gently.
It tastes the strong-smelling petrol that the captain poured in.
It tastes the fish as they leap reluctantly into the net.

Murdo Laurie (10)
Lees Hill CE Primary School, Brampton

MEMORIES OF THE MOON

Looking at the ground far below, seeing people as they go,
Looking at his star friends surrounding him.
Lighting up the sky around him
And then it goes to the old ways again,
Looking around he can see all the wonderful things
That only the stars and black sky can see.

Smelling the fish and chips and all the other good food that's
                                                    being served
And starts to feel hungry,
Smelling the ladies' perfume so sweet and lovely.
He wishes he had a lady to himself,
He knows it will never happen.

Feeling the stars beneath his feet.
Feeling the wind searching, creeping around him.
Feeling the stars tickling his toes as they dance by.

Hearing the people laughing and having fun.
Hearing the screams of people in danger.
Hearing the planes as they quickly fly by.
Hearing the boys and girls crying when they've been told off.

Madeleine Hodges (10)
Lees Hill CE Primary School, Brampton

MEMORIES OF A DOOR

A door sees two tidy rooms,
It sees them being painted bright colours.
Sees people popping in and out busily,
Sees people working at their polished desks.

A door smells people's breath, the stink of toothpaste.
It smells the aroma of coffee being made,
Smelling stinking old hamster poo,
Smells the dusty old smell of chalk.

A door feels the warm hands stroking on its wood.
It feels angry people aggressively kicking it open,
Feeling people sticking pins into it,
Feels itself click back quietly into the door frame.

A door hears the noisy talk of chattering people,
Hears the squeak of chalk sticks on the blackboard.
It hears the constant click of computer keys
And hears the grand piano playing restful tunes.

Fiona Laurie (9)
Lees Hill CE Primary School, Brampton

MEMORIES OF A ROCK

I am a rock, spying on the waves crashing on the beach,
Droplets of water splashing me.
Spying lots of feet with teeny, tiny eyes,
Spying the seagulls soaring high in the sky,
Spying the barking dogs trying to swallow me whole!

I am a rock, sniffing the salty sea air floating all around me,
Sniffing the angry birds thinking I'm a tasty snack,
Sniffing the chattering humans with my crunched-up nose,
Sniffing children having fun in the huge salty sea.

I am a rock, feeling the grains of sand that surround me like an army,
Feeling the wet seawater with my rough, wrinkled hands,
Feeling the cold air covering me with a frosty coat,
Feeling the soles of shoes treading upon my head.

I am a rock, listening to the waves suddenly crashing on the shore,
Listening to the quiet murmur of the people chattering all day long,
Listening to the gentle waves lapping the shore,
Listen . . . listen . . . listen . . .!

Jessica Betts (10)
Lees Hill CE Primary School, Brampton

MEMORIES OF A RIVER

Look at this poor river
I stare at the way it is living
Glare at its hard rock eyes
People like to mock it

Tasting the river's heavy load
It's trying to eat away the banks
Bit by bit and spitting it out
When it slows down

Smell all its dirty pollution
Smell the deliberate stench of filthy pollution
Sniff in all the badness
Which makes us realise what we've done
To this poor river

I am touching this river's heart
Which is feeling very gloomy
Make the river feel the same as we

Hear the screaming of the river
Worried about drowning in the heavy rain
Hear the whimpering of the river
Whispering softly, 'Stop, please.'

Frances Boyle (9)
Lees Hill CE Primary School, Brampton

MEMORIES OF THE BLINKING EYE BRIDGE

I am the blinking eye bridge
I can see the boats drifting under me
As I slowly tilt back to allow them through

I am the blinking eye bridge
I can taste the polluted water
As it swirls down my throat
Like little whirlpools

I am the blinking eye bridge
I can touch the frosty air as it whistles past me
It numbs my face, blue and white

I am the blinking eye bridge
I can hear the water lapping against
The side of the river
Like fish licking stone walls.

Teo Castelvecchi (8)
Lees Hill CE Primary School, Brampton

MEMORIES OF THE SEA

The sea can see the rocks plummeting towards it
The sea can see the sting from the transparent jellyfish
The sea can see swirling sand settling on the bed

The sea can see tiny drops of blood of dying fish
The sea can taste the debris of cars and bags
The sea can taste the pealing paint of the boats
The sea can taste crumbling coral of the reefs

The sea can smell the poison of the boats' petrol
The sea can smell swordfish being fried on the yacht above
The sea can smell the suntan lotion on young children

The sea can feel the jagged rocks
The sea can feel the rough sand against its soft skin
The sea can feel the ticking of fish as they scoot about

The sea can hear the rumbling of engines from boats
The sea can hear the chatter of people on board
The sea can hear the crack of the cricket ball on the bat.

Hamish Byers (9)
Lees Hill CE Primary School, Brampton

A WINDY DAY

Last night I heard on the weather forecast
There was going to be a gale
In the morning I found my windows clean open
And my curtains on the floor
I went downstairs and saw my mum and my brother
Looking out the window at the willow
Swaying dangerously in the wind
The roaring gale could be heard outside
And the howling of the wind
Suddenly the glass shattered all over the floor
We saw the wind uproar and the willow tree uprooted.

Alexandra Lee (9)
Leven Valley CE Primary School, Ulverston

THE GALE FORCE WIND

One dark night the windows rattled,
The door let in quite a scream,
I saw five trees uprooted and one house roof,
I listened, then I heard a moaning sound
Coming from the west,
I heard a howl, then a lash of wind caught me,
I shivered,
I heard a crash,
I thought that it was our house,
But it was a tree crashing onto the house
Like a hard bang on a drum.

Evelyn Wilson (8)
Leven Valley CE Primary School, Ulverston

THE WINDY DAY

One gusty day,
I went for a walk in the woods,
A tree had been ripped up,
Its roots looked like a giant's hair,
I hate wind, do you?

Kate Dickinson (7)
Leven Valley CE Primary School, Ulverston

A RECIPE FOR A POLLUTED STREAM

Take 1 stream
Just add tin cans, glass and plastic
Add bottles and bags to kill the fish
Add oil to make the stream look black
Sprinkle paper on top
Leave it to cook in the sun

This is a recipe for a polluted stream.

Liam Turner (9)
Ludworth Primary School, Ludworth

MY COOL GARDEN

Birds are singing in the trees,
On the flowers are lots of bees.
In the summer, when it is hot,
The flowers' colours are like a rainbow.
Butterflies flying in the sky,
They won't come down,
They would rather fly.

Samantha Jade Ager (8)
Ludworth Primary School, Ludworth

STOP POLLUTING THE RIVERS!

Stop polluting the rivers and streams
And *stop* putting chemicals in the water too
Please don't pollute the rivers
Because fish live there
And they can die

So *stop* polluting the water
It's not nice and it's not safe
Please save the countryside
It's not too late
So *stop* polluting rivers
It's up to me and you!

Helen Atkinson (9)
Ludworth Primary School, Ludworth

STOP!

Stop cutting down trees,
Save them to make paper!
Stop putting rubbish in the sea,
It will make life better for you and me!
Stop polluting water, it is not safe,
Save the country, it's not too late!

We are breaking the country
And that's a fact!
If you don't help us,
You'll get sacked!

Joanne Bassett (10)
Ludworth Primary School, Ludworth

WE MUST PROTECT THE COUNTRYSIDE

We must protect the countryside,
The flowers, the trees, the animals and the bees.

We must protect the countryside,
Don't throw your rotten rubbish on the ground,
Put it in a bin
And keep your dog upon a lead
And if you can't, keep it in.

We must protect the countryside,
Don't chop, chop, chop down the trees,
So you can sell it in a shop,
Wrapping up the cheddar cheese.

We must protect the countryside,
Remember it is *ours!*

Amy Heseltine (11)
Ludworth Primary School, Ludworth

PLEASE

P   lease
L   eave
E   verything living alone!
A   ll of us should walk, not pollute by driving
    through our countryside
S   omeone has to stop our factories,
    it is us!
E   veryone should help keep our world clean
    and don't forget the ocean.

Yasmin Couto (10)
Ludworth Primary School, Ludworth

OUTSIDE MY HOME

Dark, dusty sky
Shiny moonlight
Shining down on a foggy night
Stars twinkle like gold treasure

Blue sky looking down like the ocean
Green grass growing
Shiny golden sky like a light
Millions of clouds covering us all

White, silky snow covering
The ground of every street
Animals hiding in their homes
People sitting in front of a warm fire.

Dean Winter (9)
Ludworth Primary School, Ludworth

DIZZY

I'm so, so dizzy
I can't even see
What is around me.
All I can see is . . .
An empty space,
Full of rubbish.
'What a disgrace.'
It is a bike . . . no wheels . . .
No handlebars . . .
All I can say is it looks like Mars,
So why do you pollute the air with cars?
Don't you want to see the
Stars!

Craig Hall (9)
Ludworth Primary School, Ludworth

KEEPING THINGS SAFE

Please protect the country,
The animals and trees,
All of the flowers and
The buzzing bees.
Don't throw litter in the lakes,
Keep it in a bin,
Then we'll be safe.

Help protect the animals,
Don't frighten them away.
They belong in their homes,
Grass or hay.
Empty glass bottles smashed and crushed,
Please protect the country . . .
It's up to *us!*

Natasha Ager (9)
Ludworth Primary School, Ludworth

MY LOVELY HOME

I love my home
It's like a dome
I love my home when I go outside

The wind flows
My dad mows

In the kitchen
My mam is baking a cake
We like to eat the cakes she makes.

Scott Carter (8)
Ludworth Primary School, Ludworth

PROTECT OUR WORLD

Please don't make our world bad!
It will make you sad!
With nothing to do!
Please keep our sky blue!
Do not slice our trees down
Or the animals will frown!
Do not pollute our water!
All of our underwater daughters will die!
So say goodbye.

Samantha Stones (10)
Ludworth Primary School, Ludworth

THE WINDY GARDEN

The wind in my garden is very strong
It moves the trees as it whistles along
The plants move to and fro
The petals fall around
Landing everywhere on the ground
The clothes on the line are blowing wild
They go up and down and hit the floor
They sometimes blow next door.

Jonathan Sutherland (8)
Ludworth Primary School, Ludworth

THE FANTASTIC GARDEN

My garden is so lovely
It's full of flowers and trees
The trees are good for the birds
And the flowers are good for the bees

My garden is so lovely
The trees are lovely and green
People say they are the best
That they have ever seen.

Ryan Hall (7)
Ludworth Primary School, Ludworth

WHAT I CAN SEE

In my garden, the trees are big
The grass is long, the ground is alive
Butterflies and bees flying free

Chickens walking freely
Many eggs gathered by my mum
Such a busy garden
But as night falls
Everything is so peaceful.

Kate Critchlow (7)
Ludworth Primary School, Ludworth

MY BACK GARDEN

At the end of the garden, there is a big hole,
My back fence is slimy,
There is rubbish in the garden,
I look out of the window,
I can see the broken chairs and tables,
I have burnt wood all over,
I don't like my garden.

Keiran Steward (9)
Ludworth Primary School, Ludworth

MOUNTAIN

Water
Flows
Down
Water gets
Polluted
Ozone dies
Animals shrink
Animals die
Try to climb it
Sometimes die
Made of rocks
Grass with ice
Don't pollute the water
In case you kill the animals.

Kieryn Heseltine (9)
Ludworth Primary School, Ludworth

MY GARDEN

Twittering, chattering birds
Bright blue sky
Glittering, glistening grass
Shiny coloured flowers
Blowing breezy trees

I like to play in my wonderful garden
Birds building their nests
White, smoky clouds looking down at my
Beautiful garden.

Zoe Stones (8)
Ludworth Primary School, Ludworth

THE FANTASTIC GARDEN

I like to sit in my garden on a nice hot, sunny day,
Sometimes I just sit there and sometimes I will play,
The flowers are so pretty when they bloom,
Sometimes I pick them and put them in my room,
The fountain is so lovely, it makes a trickling sound,
It makes me want to sit there on the stony ground.

Rebekah Hall (8)
Ludworth Primary School, Ludworth

MY WICKED GARDEN

My garden has small trees
And nuts to feed the birds
The flowers smell lovely
Bright green grass and cabbages
The caterpillars eat the cabbages, yum, yum
They live in my little garden.

Jonathan Kell (8)
Ludworth Primary School, Ludworth

WATERFALL

Sparkling jewels spray down the mountain,
Thrashing rapids bounce down over the rocks,
The pressure whipping down,
Water crushes against the rocks,
The river floods its banks,
The waterfall shoots into the mudflats.

Joseph Barkhouse (10)
Maryport CE Junior School, Maryport

TIDYING THE BEDROOM

Click! Creak! Whoosh! - Door slowly opening.
Scream! Screech! - Mum screaming at the mess.
Boom! Clank! Clink! - Emptying the bookshelf.
Swish! Swash! Swoosh! - Dusting the furniture.
Whoo! Whoo! Whoo! - Hoovering the carpet.
Whoosh! Whoosh! Whoosh! - Putting clean sheets on the bed.

Sparkle! Sparkle! Shimmer! - The bedroom *is* tidy.

Paige Graham (9)
Maryport CE Junior School, Maryport

WATER

I run down rivers into the glittering sea,
I am the ice to skate and the snow to ski.

I am the liquid in the washer to help you clean your pants
And the liquid from the sky that helps to grow the plants.

Sometimes, I am the roaring, raving white horses in the sea
And some other times, I can be as calm as can be!

Carl Joseph Wilson (10)
Maryport CE Junior School, Maryport

FIRE

I begin my life in many ways and often last for several days,
I am hot, orange, black and blue,
With poisonous smoke that could choke you.
I tear through buildings as quick as a flash
And end my life in a pile of ash.

Daniel Brannon (11)
Maryport CE Junior School, Maryport

THE WHALE

The whale is a skyscraper sunken in the sea,
It is a tidal wave come to swallow me.
The whale is a silhouette frozen in the air,
It is a battle of conflict thrashing without care.
The whale is a black, dark December night,
It is an inky monster coming to give a fright.
The whale is a skyscraper sunken in the sea,
It is a tidal wave come to swallow me.

Robyn Clements (11)
Maryport CE Junior School, Maryport

WATER!

Can you hear the water
As it drips down a drain?
Can you hear it flowing
As it flows down the lane
It's good to have water,
As you may not be alive,
But you've got to be careful not to drink dirty water,
As you may not survive!

Jay Oglanby (10)
Maryport CE Junior School, Maryport

THE DRAGON

The dragon has giant, golden eyes,
Two silent wings, which flap in the billowing air.
The dragon has scales all over its body,
Nails like spears and pointed ears,
Sharp teeth and a long jagged tail.

Charlotte Easterbrook (10)
Maryport CE Junior School, Maryport

THE HIGHWAYMAN

The highwayman is tall and dark
With soft, blond hair,
His face is scarred, it's like a punctured tyre,
He has a ghostly personality,
He wears a red velvet coat,
With long boots, he is like an undertaker,
He is as cunning as a fox,
He's king of the highway.

John Ritson (9)
Maryport CE Junior School, Maryport

EATING BREAKFAST

Hubble, hubble (the kettle's boiling)
Pop (out comes the toast)
Scrape, scratch (spreading the butter)
Splish, splash (putting the cereal into the bowl)
Ding (the spoon hitting the bowl)
Smacking and slurping (of the lips)
Patting (of tummies, all full up).

Anna Mulgrew (10)
Maryport CE Junior School, Maryport

IF I WASN'T WHO I AM

If I wasn't who I am, I would swim a thousand miles.
If I wasn't who I am, I would go for football trials.
If I wasn't who I am, I would dance around the moon.
If I wasn't who I am, I would sing a little tune.
But I am who I am - a loving, caring child.
I am Megan.

Megan Murdock (10)
Maryport CE Junior School, Maryport

SIBERIAN TIGER

Tiger,
A cunning, speedy, silent beast.
Creeping,
Sleeping,
Hunting, sprinting, pouncing on its prey,
Camouflaged in the sunlight.

Tiger,
A colossal, beautiful, powerful cat,
Attacking,
Devouring,
Chasing, tearing, bolting across the African plains,
Stalking twenty herds of gazelle.

Tiger,
An amazing, mighty, ravenous animal,
Almost extinct,
Helpful thief,
She's a loving mother, feeding her cubs,
Her thundering roar rattles the land.

Beware! The Siberian tiger.

Sophie Marsden (9)
Maryport CE Junior School, Maryport

THE SPIDER

I can climb any wall or lampshade,
I can crawl all over you when you bathe.
I can scare little children, then they will *scream!*
I can hide in a corner with my team.
I can crawl all day until it is night,
Then I'll start again when dark becomes light.

Stephen Tunstall (10)
Maryport CE Junior School, Maryport

Rain

Trickle, trickle on my hand,
Running down my leg;
As I walk, the water splashes,
Like silvery droplets, falling down,
Running down my spine,
I look up, what do I see?
I see little lines, one little bit,
I bet you know what I see,
Yes I see rain,
It's raining rain,
It's raining rain,
It's raining rain.

Dominick Southwell (9)
Maryport CE Junior School, Maryport

The Mermaid

The deep blue ocean,
Rising up,
Crashing down on all the rocks.

All of a sudden,
A big, big *splash,*
A mermaid appears with shiny scales.

Her scales turn gold,
When they are caught in the sun,
But she jumps back in and swims right down
To the bottom of the deep blue sea.

Rachel Parker (9)
Maryport CE Junior School, Maryport

CHINA DOLL

I wear a pink-flowered gown,
With silver lining going down.
I wear a cream-beaded shawl,
For I am a china doll.

I have a pot china face,
A cream bonnet lined with lace,
In my hand I hold a scroll,
For I am a china doll.

If you need a dear friend,
I will be with you to the end,
You can name me Moll or Poll,
For I am your china doll.

Emily McCracken (10)
Maryport CE Junior School, Maryport

FEAR

Fear is cold and dark,
It eats nasty creatures,
It makes you jump back into bed.

Fear creeps up behind you,
It jumps into your heart,
Fear is horrible,
It lives inside *you.*

Hayley Howard (10)
Maryport CE Junior School, Maryport

SWEETS

Sweets, sweets, sweets, the things that I adore,
Sweets, sweets, sweets, I want more and more and more.
Strawberry, apple, raspberry, pineapple,
Blueberry, melon, gooseberry, lemon,
Black grape, mango, white grape, tango,
Blackberry, plum, red berry, run.
Sweets, sweets, sweets, come in every flavour,
Sweets, sweets, sweets, the things that I love to savour.
Yellow, green, aquamarine,
Canary, emerald and serene.
Sweets, sweets, sweets are very, very colourful,
Sweets, sweets, sweets are both bright and doleful.

Kamay Li (10)
Mowden Junior School, Darlington

THE RUGBY GAME

The rugby game commenced
As the players came out
But one had to go over the fence
All the fans shout
Lots of players fall
They run across the muddy pitch
It was a rubbish mall
So I think rugby is a brilliant game
But my mum doesn't think the same!

Hannah Sykes (11)
Mowden Junior School, Darlington

WINTER WEATHER

Wind is whistling in the night,
It's dancing around the lamp post so bright,
Climbing the sky, using its claws,
Up, up and up it soars,
Into the heart of Heaven above.

Frost is icing the window closed,
Rosy-red cheeks and a frostbitten nose,
He's gliding along, making everything freeze,
He's dancing around, making everyone sneeze,
The world's wishing he'd have a rest,
Jack Frost is being a pest.

Jessica Hawthorn (10)
Mowden Junior School, Darlington

THE MIGHTY JUNGLE

From branch to branch they swing,
The mighty jungle call, the monkeys sing.
The hissing snake curls its winding scales,
Round the trunks like the monkeys' tails.
The spider crawls over a bed of leaves,
Behind an ant, grain it heaves.
The toucan flutters through the air,
Passing trees and a grizzly bear.
In the corner, the lion spies,
Slaughtered meat and irritating flies.

Kate Sayer (11)
Mowden Junior School, Darlington

THE MAGIC BOX

I will put in the box . . .
The swish of a black horse's tail,
The gallop of an Indian's horse through an enchanted forest,
A spark from a ball of fire.

I will put in the box . . .
The very last howl from a wolf,
The darkest place in the universe,
Two small hops from a white rabbit.

I will put in the box . . .
The black and white stripes of a zebra,
Three magic books in a tortoise's shell,
A graceful purple and gold bird from Heaven.

I will put in the box . . .
The sound of a cricket rubbing his wings together,
The thirteenth month called Iramenth,
Two pearls in a shell.

My box is sparkling purple, with a glistening green lock and key,
It's got secrets on the bottom and the hinges are made of sugar lumps.

Seraphina Kelvey-Brown (11)
Mowden Junior School, Darlington

ICE

Icicles hug the windowpanes,
His frosty face is looking glazed,
As log fires glow,
Here comes the first snow,
It covers the garden in a blanket,
It hugs the top of the mountains.

Duncan Turner (10)
Mowden Junior School, Darlington

WOLF

It creeps around the woods at night
Scaring birds so they take flight
Howling at the midnight moon
The Grand Wolf Hunt will take place soon
A swishing tail sweeps through the leaves
It hopes some prey it will receive
As its gleaming eyes catch moonlight beams
Cute face, not always what it seems
Howling at the midnight moon
The Grand Wolf Hunt will take place soon.

Bethany Simpson (11)
Mowden Junior School, Darlington

IT WASN'T ME!

It wasn't me who stole your chocolate
It just appeared round my mouth!
It wasn't me who broke the vase
It just jumped off the shelf!
It wasn't me who messed up my room
It did it by itself!
It wasn't me who dirtied my shirt
It just dived in the mud!
It wasn't me I swear!
By the way, where is my teddy bear?
. . . It wasn't me!

Hannah Garbutt (10)
Mowden Junior School, Darlington

THE ICE PLANET

Ice boulder swerving lava
Shooting down ice mountains
Striking blue thunder
Out of the ice sky
Venus, planet of ice rivers
Blue fireworks zooming
Roads of ice.

Luke Stephenson (6)
Plumpton School, Penrith

ANIMALS

Some pets are furry,
But some are purry,
Cats like to sunbathe,
Some dogs are called Dave.

Bears like to eat honey,
Owls have lots of money,
Most live in your house,
The cat has found a mouse.

You can get them as a cuddly toy,
Even for a boy!
Kittens are very small,
Giraffes are very tall!

Pets you can find in a pet shop
Some can be found in a mop!
Some only come out at night
Because they don't like the light.

Rachel Huck (10)
Ravenstonedale Endowed School, Kirkby Stephen

SPRING

Spring is silent and sweet,
Solemn and neat.

Flowers bud beautiful and bright,
Soaking up the sunlight.

The tree returns to life with a heart that's kind
And leaves return to the colour of green.

Every animal that seems to have been lost,
Is reunited without any cost.

Lambs are born like clouds of joy,
They skip around like a playful toy.

Easter arrives with cheeks a-glowing,
Easter eggs for the showing.

Then spring goes to sleep,
Summer begins to come in with a leap.

Hannah Mason (9)
Ravenstonedale Endowed School, Kirkby Stephen

MY HAMSTER

My hamster crawls around
Without making a sound
It's here and there
It climbs up the bars on the house
Through the tube, up the ladder
That's what it will do forever and ever!

Claire Huck (7)
Ravenstonedale Endowed School, Kirkby Stephen

JACQUELINE WILSON

Jacqueline Wilson is just simply the best,
She'd beat all authors in a test.
For a girl, her writing is so exciting,
For a boy, she gives some joy.
The Illustrated Mum is just the tops,
Jacqueline pulls out all the stops.
Every night while I'm tucked up tight,
I read her books,
While my mum cooks.
Tracy Beaker, Dolphin and Star,
They're my favourites, they've gone so far.

Molly Livesey (9)
Ravenstonedale Endowed School, Kirkby Stephen

THINGS I LIKE

I like shopping with my mates,
Eating pizzas off clean plates.
I like music and CDs,
Hiding my mum and dad's car keys.
I like high-heeled sandals, trainers too
And walking up the avenue.
I like the beach on a sunny day
And going to a posh hotel to stay.
My favourite sport is rollerblading,
I like my jeans when the knees are fading.

Emma Staley (9)
Ravenstonedale Endowed School, Kirkby Stephen

FIELDS OF GOLD!

Rushing winds of strong big blows,
Makes wheat wave in green meadows.
Flowers blooming and crops a-rising,
See the cows and sheep start smiling.
Winter's gone and spring has come,
Upon the fields of gold.
There is now a colour of shining light,
As the sun has come and left the night.
Around us we can see the way
Of grassy fields gay.
Animals eat the field's grass,
Up in the field of gold.
When spring has gone and summer's here,
That fresh farm won't disappear.

Mckenzie Powell (8)
Ravenstonedale Endowed School, Kirkby Stephen

STORM

Lightning flashes
Thunder crashes
Above our heads

Horrible, scary noise
Jump! went all the boys
Who were playing with their toys

Rain splatters down
Pitter-patter sound
Soaks the ground.

Calum Hopps (10)
Ravenstonedale Endowed School, Kirkby Stephen

CATS

Cats on the piano,
Cats on the floor,
Cats on the patio,
Cats by the door,
Cats on the sofa,
Cats on the ledge,
Cats in the middle,
Cats on the edge.

> Cats on the curtains,
> Cats in a cardboard box,
> Cats on the table
> Or in the cupboard with your frocks!
> Cats on your papers,
> Cats on the telly,
> Cats on the mantelpiece,
> Cats on your belly!

Cats in your knicker drawer,
Cats in your socks,
Cats on the video game
Or sitting in your homework box!
Cats on the coffee table,
Cats on the chair,
Cats on the lampshade,
Cats *everywhere!*

Samantha Dent (10)
Ravenstonedale Endowed School, Kirkby Stephen

PLAYGROUND

The cars are screeching, the children are screaming.
The balls are bouncing.
The children are falling and shouting.
A child is dashing, the bins are clashing.

The birds are chirping.
The parents are talking.
The prams are rattling.
The bell is ringing.

Nicholas Todd (10)
St Cuthbert's RC Primary School, Chester-Le-Street

WISH, WISH, WISH

I wish that I wouldn't forget.
I wish my brother wasn't obsessed with cars.
I wish I had another pet.
I wish I could go on a trip to Mars.

I wish my brother wasn't here.
I wish I had blonde hair.
I wish my dad wouldn't drink beer.
I wish I could meet a grizzly bear.

I wish my teeth were straight.
I wish my freckles would go.
I wish I could stay up really late.
I wish I could see a magic show.

I wish I could watch my favourite cartoon.
I wish my brother would run away.
I wish I could walk on the moon.
I wish I could go on holiday.

I wish I didn't go to school.
I wish I had more video games.
I wish I had an ice cream swimming pool.
I wish I could remember more names.

Rebecca Quinn (9)
St Cuthbert's RC Primary School, Chester-Le-Street

FIREWORK FUN

Boom, zoom, boom, whee, whizz
The spectacular fireworks cry out
The Catherine wheel goes round
Babies cry, people buy
Sparkles sizzle and zizzle
'Oh, ah,' shout the crowd
Boom, zoom, crinkle, fizzle
The fireworks still go on
Crinkle, sizzle, hiss
The bonfire whispers
Lighting up the way
People calling friends and family over
Babies crying, waa, waa, waa
Dogs woofing, cats yapping
The fireworks still go on
The sky is lit up
But the Catherine wheel still goes round
'Ooh, ooh,' say the crowd
And at the end of the display, the sky is dark
And all you can hear is the owl hooting
The cloud moves silently away
And the moon lights up the path
All you see is the cat miaowing
The sky is dark again
And all you can hear is the owl hooting.

Rachel Towers (10)
St Cuthbert's RC Primary School, Chester-Le-Street

OUT AT PLAY

Out at play you hear children laughing, ha, ha, ha.
Out at play you hear children crying, waa, waa, waa.
Out at play you hear children shouting, yeah, yeah, yeah!
Out at play you hear children's feet, patter, patter, patter.

Out at play you hear children shouting, 'Bet you can't get me.'
Out at play you hear dinner ladies shouting, 'Gulp, gulp, gulp, now!'
Bell goes, children running, pitter, pitter, patter.
Quickly, hurry up, bell's gone, ding-dong, ding-dong.

Shauna Richardson (10)
St Cuthbert's RC Primary School, Chester-Le-Street

THE GRAVEYARD AT NIGHT

It's 12 o'clock at night
Beep! goes my watch
Tu-whit tu-whoo goes an owl
Trrrt goes a grasshopper
Aaaaaaah
What was that?
A zombie rises out of the ground!
'Aaaaaaah' it moans
It squelches as it moves
'Aaaaaaah' I scream and run away
Hawoooo, oh no, it sounds like a werewolf
Am I dreaming? I pinch myself
Ow! It hurt, I'm awake, it is real!
I'm at a metal fence, I want out!
Clang! Clink! Clong! I hit the fence with an iron torch
Aaaaaah! The zombie's getting closer!
I hit it with the torch and
Squelch, the headless zombie
Dong! Clang! A hole is in the fence
Ch! Ch! My shoes slap the concrete ground as I run
Creak! I open the front door, step in and -
Slam!

Sean Winnie (10)
St Cuthbert's RC Primary School, Chester-Le-Street

WISH, WISH, WISH

I wish I could give a great big scare
I wish that I could shoot to Mars
I wish I could run everywhere
I wish I could go to play with the stars

I wish I could have a really good dream
I wish I could do a really good dance
I wish, I wish I could go on a train with some steam
I wish I could go on a holiday to France

I wish that I could go on a boat
I wish I could fly high in the sky
I wish I was able to swim and float
I wish I could bake an apple pie

I wish I was as small as a mouse
I wish I could have nicer hair
I wish I could have my own little house
I wish that I would actually care

I wish that I could have a pet cat
I wish I had a gel pen range
I wish I could wear a top hat
I wish that me, my life would change.

Rachel Lilley (8)
St Cuthbert's RC Primary School, Chester-Le-Street

SWIMMING

The waves crash and splash
The diving board cracks and screeches
The children splash and giggle
The water jumps and creaks
The water drips and bangs

The children run, patter, patter, patter
The lifeguard shouts, 'Errr'
The ball swooshes in the air
The buzzer rings, *buzzzzz*
It's time to go.

Daniel Graham (11)
St Cuthbert's RC Primary School, Chester-Le-Street

WISH, WISH, WISH

I wish I had a good chance to ski,
I wish my hat was not so wet,
I wish I could meet my good friend Lee,
I wish I had a really fat debt

I wish Samantha was not such a pig,
I wish I could learn something new,
I wish Catherine could try to dig,
I wish I could make a tasty stew.

I wish I had every single toy,
I wish I was a really good swimmer,
I wish I knew just one more boy,
I wish my job was not to serve dinner.

I wish I owned one little pet,
I wish there was no such thing as school,
I wish I owned a turbo jet,
I wish I could go swimming in a diving pool.

I wish I had a nice big house,
I wish I had relatives that lived in igloos,
I wish I knew a talking mouse,
I wish I could always watch Scooby-Doo.

Alex Brown (9)
St Cuthbert's RC Primary School, Chester-Le-Street

IN A FARMYARD

In a farmyard
You might hear . . .
The cluck and croak and groan
Of the chickens bawling
The baa and bleat and blump
Of the sheep snorting
The moo and the moan and strone
Of the cows crowning
The snorting and sniffing and squealing
Of the pigs ponging
The neighing and norting and nork
Of the horses horting
The gibble and groan and gobble
Of the goats gibbling
The bark and babble and bellow
Of the dogs drooling
But . . .
When the farmer goes to bed
All is silent.

Hannah Roberts (9)
St Cuthbert's RC Primary School, Chester-Le-Street

FIREWORKS

Crackle, fizz, clang
The bonfire goes bang
Hiss, whizz, zoom
The fireworks go boom

Sausages sizzling
Baked beans burning
All in the light
Of the bonfires gloom

I love fireworks
So do my friends
They're so noisy
They'll get you out of your beds!

Sam Owens (9)
St Cuthbert's RC Primary School, Chester-Le-Street

WISH, WISH, WISH

I wish I had a pet bunny.
I wish I wasn't really sad.
I wish I was really funny.
I wish I didn't feel bad.

I wish I wasn't very shy.
I wish I wasn't really smelly.
I wish I was really sly.
I wish I didn't have a big fat belly.

I wish I had a cuddly pet.
I wish my eyes were blue.
I wish I wasn't really wet.
I wish I had a name called Sue.

I wish I wasn't really small.
I wish my hair wasn't so frizzy.
I wish I knew how to kick a ball.
I wish my life wasn't so busy.

I wish I was in a gang.
I wish I was really groovy.
I wish I could speak slang.
I wish I could stay up late and watch a movie.

Joshua Carr (8)
St Cuthbert's RC Primary School, Chester-Le-Street

HIDDEN IN THE SCHOOL

Underneath the floorboards
Where the carpet stops
There's a sound that's curious
Sounds like clippety-clops
The school children hear it
There's a certain smell that reeks
I think we have a thousand mice
Because I can hear squeaks
Then move into the dinner hall
Dinner ladies with flip-flops
Hear the popcorn shouting
Pop! Plop! Pop!
Now into the toilets
Pull the chain and flush
I am wet all over
I'll have to get a brush
Now let's wash our hands
Quick, grab the soap
Squiggle, squaggle, squirm
Bubble, bubble, pop!

Roisin Cook (10)
St Cuthbert's RC Primary School, Chester-Le-Street

THE PLAYGROUND

Parents were chatting, feet were rattling
Children scream and shout
Babies crying, balls flying
Children playing football, screaming when scoring
Birds chirping sweetly in their nests
Cars rushing and Mr Lish pushing the bins out.

Alan Stokoe (9)
St Cuthbert's RC Primary School, Chester-Le-Street

AT THE ZOO

At the zoo, it's starting to rain
Plip, plop, splash, plip, plop, splash
At the desk, paying the lady
Tinkle, tinkle, plonk, our change rolling away

At the giraffe pen, it's lunchtime for them
Munch, munch, crunch, munch, munch, crunch
Babies screaming, scared of the big giraffes
Wailing, crying, sighing

Decided it's lunchtime in the café
Clatter of folks, clinking of plates
Sit down at the table
Scraping of chairs, munching of food

In the penguin house
Splish, splash, splosh
In the dolphin arena
Ooing and aahing.

Out in the fresh air
Wind whistling by
By the ice cream van
Slurp, slurp, slurp

In the zoo shop
Erring, as we decide what to buy
Back to the car
Snoring and sighing.

Katie Whitehead (10)
St Cuthbert's RC Primary School, Chester-Le-Street

BATH TIME

Whoosh! Splish! Splosh! (In goes water)
Glug! Glug! Glug! (Bubble bath squirting in)
Tinkle! Tinkle! (Go the bath salts)
Whoosh! (Off goes my top, landing in the sink)
Zziipp! (Down go trousers)
Bang! (Me jumping into the bath, loudly)
Aaahh . . . (Me relaxing in the lovely bath)
Ping! Pong! (That silly soap sliding into the bath)
Splish! Splosh! Whizz! Bang! Clatter! Wallop! Pop! (Me trying to catch the soap)
Gotcha! (Me catching the soap)
We will, we will rock you! (Me singing so badly)
Bang! (Me actually jumping out of the bath)
Creak . . . (My mum coming in to se what all the noise is about)
Tut! Tut! Tut! (My mum looking around at the mess)
Scrich! Scratch! (Me drying myself)
Glug! Glug! (Water tinkling down the drain . . .)

Kate Riddler (9)
St Cuthbert's RC Primary School, Chester-Le-Street

BATH TIME

(Swoosh, swish) there goes the water into the bath
(Plop, plop, oh) there go my feet into the bath and myself
(La, la, la, oh) Relaxing in the water
(Whish, whoosh) me pouring the water over my hair
(La, la, la, la) me singing in the bath
(Swish, swoosh, squirt) squirting the shampoo on my hair
(Whish, whoosh) me rinsing my hair
(Gurgle, gurgle) me letting the plug out of the bath
(Plop, plop, whoosh) me getting out of the bath
(Rub, rub, ah) I'm getting dried with the towel, it's lovely.

Carmen Citrone (11)
St Cuthbert's RC Primary School, Chester-Le-Street

THE FAIRGROUND

At the fairground, when I'm at the entrance,
I hear music from the merry-go-round,
I go there and see people and children laughing,
In the distance I hear people screaming,
Whee! On the roller coaster ride
And trundle off the wheels.
I see smiling faces,
People old or young,
Having a really good time.
People slurping, having a drink,
Sizzles of hot dogs cooking.
Bang! Clatter! Something breaking,
All too soon, it's time to go home,
The roaring of the engine
And off we go!

Claire Williamson (9)
St Cuthbert's RC Primary School, Chester-Le-Street

FIREWORK NIGHT

Boom, bang, crash, sizzle, bash go the fireworks,
People say that the ghost of Guy Fawkes lurks,
Chatter, chitter, chat, chit, chat; everybody's amazed
Oh! Ah! They are lovely! People gazed
Whoosh! Whizz! Zoom, they zoom across the sky
Waa, waa, wail, wail, babies cry
Tonight everything is loud in the streets
Munch, crunch, yum, yum, yum, everybody eats
Wee, dee, zoom, the Catherine wheel cries
Tonight it's so noisy and all the sparks fly.

Alexandra White (9)
St Cuthbert's RC Primary School, Chester-Le-Street

MYSTERY!

Walking through the woods, day has gone, night has come.
Crunch, snap, oops, I stood on some twigs.
Whoosh, whoosh, whoosh go the leaves as I rustle through them.
Whip, whoosh, whoop, down swoops the owl and lands on my shoulder.
Hoot, hoot is the owl trying to tell me something?
I turn around, ah, I gasp while drawing my breath.
Boop, bang, 'Help,' I scream as a witch drags me along the
                                        damp wood floor.
What is she going to do with me?
'Ha, ha, ha, ha, ha.'
The witch is cackling
And that's a bad sign . . .

Emily Thompson (10)
St Cuthbert's RC Primary School, Chester-Le-Street

THE PLAYGROUND

I hear the children running around
Someone is crying, they fell on the ground
Throwing a ball
Doing nothing at all
All of a sudden, the bell starts to ring
At the end of the ring, there is a ping
In the middle of school, there is a van
Someone comes in, they have a tan
The birds are singing in the trees
What's that buzzing?
Oh it's the bees.

Tom Scurfield (9)
St Cuthbert's RC Primary School, Chester-Le-Street

THE FAIRGROUND

Whee! Go the children on the rides,
Whoo! Go the people on the slides.
Yeah! Go the adults on 'Hook the duck',
Oh no! Go the people without any luck.
Yum, yum! Go the kids eating candyfloss,
Yoohoo! Go the parents, their children are a loss.
Splash! Go the logs with families in,
Dump! Goes the rubbish being dumped in the bin!
Yippee! Go the children having fun,
Hello! Goes a lady, watching her son.
Ah! Go the people on the roller coaster, hear them scream,
Wow! The jewels in the lucky dip gleam.
Mmm! I love the smell of hot dogs,
Oh! I want to go on the logs.

Amy Batey (10)
St Cuthbert's RC Primary School, Chester-Le-Street

AT THE ZOO

Snap! Goes the crocodile trying to get a fish,
Roar! Goes the lion king yawning away,
Thump! Goes the kangaroo jumping playfully,
Hiss! Goes the cobra attacking a mouse,
Trumpeting the elephant goes about his usual business
Neigh! Goes the zebra frolicking in the paddock,
Twitter, twitter, cheep! Go the singing birds high up in the trees,
Whoosh go the bats, zooming in the air
And giggle, giggle from the children
Laughing at the monkeys!

Grace Evans (9)
St Cuthbert's RC Primary School, Chester-Le-Street

THE SEASIDE

Clash! Go the waves,
Smash! Go the rocks,
Playing in the pool,
Ah! It's lovely and cool,
I go to sleep,
Out comes a crab,
It starts to peep,
Smack! Waves collide off my face,
'Oi!' shouts the lifeguard,
Get out that pool,
Ow! Slip on a sharp stone,
Time to go.
Bye-bye!

Nicholas McCarthy (9)
St Cuthbert's RC Primary School, Chester-Le-Street

THE PLAYGROUND

Parents chatter, babies clatter,
Children playing tig,
They're shouting, stamping, panting,
Brrrroom, room, brrr, brrrrr . . . what's that noise?
Cars are stuck in traffic,
Everyone's having a panic.
Babies crying and gurgling, why, oh why, oh why?
But then suddenly ding-a-ling-a-ling,
There's the bell,
Everyone rushes to their line!

Yasmin Lazaro (9)
St Cuthbert's RC Primary School, Chester-Le-Street

AT THE ZOO

At the zoo you hear elephants washing,
Spray, spray, spray.

But you never hear any horses,
Neigh, neigh, neigh.

At the zoo you see giraffes,
Stretch up tall.

At the zoo you see seals,
Playing with a ball.

You hear children laughing,
Ha, ha, ha.

You hear children crying,
Waa, waa, waa.

You hear penguins squeak,
Eek, eek, eek.

You hear bears trying to escape,
Creak, creak, creak.

Thallia-Ann Sheblee (10)
St Cuthbert's RC Primary School, Chester-Le-Street

ST CUTHBERT'S SCHOOL

Children shouting and calling names
And in the playground playing games
All the children have lots of fun
In St Cuthbert's School, it's mostly sun
St Cuthbert's is a Catholic school
But still I tell you, it is cool.

Patrick Cumiskey (10)
St Cuthbert's RC Primary School, Chester-Le-Street

WISH, WISH, WISH

I wish I was good at art.
I wish I had a pet dog.
I wish I could tell my friends apart.
I wish I had never got lost in the fog.

I wish I could win the lottery.
I wish I was eighteen.
I wish I was good at pottery.
I wish my friend wasn't mean.

I wish that I could drive.
I wish I had a lilac dress.
I wish that my grandad was alive.
I wish I didn't make a mess.

I wish I could bathe in the sun.
I wish I had a pet.
I wish I could have a lot of fun.
I wish I could catch a fish in a net.

I wish I could go to the beach.
I wish I had a big car.
I wish that I could teach.
I wish I didn't get stuck in the tar.

Danielle Nicholson (9)
St Cuthbert's RC Primary School, Chester-Le-Street

SWIMMING

The waves crash and scrunch ready to munch
The children crackle and splash
When something crackles and crunches something breaks
When someone gets hurt you hear bangs and screams

You hear screeching when you turn on the shower
The children walking along the side of the water, slip, slide and crash
The lifeguard screams and shouts
The diving board whistles and rattles like a volcano.

Matthew Trevena (10)
St Cuthbert's RC Primary School, Chester-Le-Street

WISH, WISH, WISH

I wish I had golden hair,
I wish I could fly,
I wish I had a giant teddy bear,
I wish I didn't always cry.

I wish my sister wasn't here,
I wish I had a big pet,
I wish my dad didn't drink so much beer,
I wish I had a great big play set.

I wish I had a fluffy cat,
I wish I could play all day in the sand,
I wish I didn't have to wear a woolly hat,
I wish I could watch a band.

I wish my sister flew to Mars,
I wish she never would return,
I wish I could drive some cars,
I wish my house wouldn't burn.

I wish I didn't always fall down,
I wish I had a great big house,
I wish I was a happy clown,
I wish I was a mouse.

Sophie Eames (8)
St Cuthbert's RC Primary School, Chester-Le-Street

THE PLAYGROUND

Before school starts Mr Lish clatters the bins
As he puts them in place
Mums chattering and babies laughing
Children run in the rustling leaves playing tig
Screech, screech go the cars as they go by
Toddlers going into playschool
Ting-a-ling-a-ling, it's time to go into school.

Jake Barker (9)
St Cuthbert's RC Primary School, Chester-Le-Street

THE PLAYGROUND

Children running around
Mums and dads chatting
Birds flying off the ground
Leaves rustling on the trees
Cars go brum, brum as parents drop off their children
I hear ring, ring, there goes the bell
Children's feet go thump, thump as they run to their lines.

Kirsty Bradley (10)
St Cuthbert's RC Primary School, Chester-Le-Street

FIREWORKS

I was watching fireworks but one scared me
Because the firework squealed and screeched
I saw a large sparkly, crackly firework in the air
There are big and small fireworks in big and small boxes
There are big, sparkly, crackly, bumpy and whistling fireworks
Fireworks crash and make large fires.

John Morgan (11)
St Cuthbert's RC Primary School, Chester-Le-Street

THE PLAYGROUND

Parents are talking while children are walking,
Babies screaming and the sun is gleaming,
Birds are chirping, toddlers murmuring,
Girls are clapping, boys are laughing,
Then you hear a beep, beep, beep,
Because the children are crossing the street,
Then, what's that? It's the bell ringing,
So the children are stamping to their lines.

Rebecca Rhys-Evans (9)
St Cuthbert's RC Primary School, Chester-Le-Street

THE PLAYGROUND

Before school parents gathering children laughing
Bushes rustling with birds humming
Balls bouncing up and down
Children shouting all around
The bell is ringing and children are singing.

Caroline Carlyle Smith (10)
St Cuthbert's RC Primary School, Chester-Le-Street

THE PLAYGROUND

Mr Lish rattling the bins in the frosty weather,
Parents chattering altogether,
Children laughing all day long,
Babies crying, balls bouncing,
Bells ring, people run.

Owen McArdle (10)
St Cuthbert's RC Primary School, Chester-Le-Street

WISH, WISH, WISH

I wish I could go on a plane.
I wish I could rollerblade.
I wish I was insane.
I wish I had a braid.

I wish I was scientific.
I wish I could shop.
I wish I could be terrific.
I wish I had a crop top.

I wish I could fly.
I wish I could have a friend.
I wish I could lie.
I wish I could go round the bend.

I wish I was 10.
I wish I could go in the past.
I wish I had a pet hen.
I wish I didn't have a cast.

I wish I got some post.
I wish I didn't care.
I wish I could go to the coast.
I wish I had a secret lair.

Jennifer Wheatley (9)
St Cuthbert's RC Primary School, Chester-Le-Street

THE PLAYGROUND

The children are playing tig
The adults are talking
Be careful, the adults are saying to their children
The children are giggling and laughing as they are walking

The caretaker takes out the bins before school
Rattles along the path they go
Ding-a-ling-a-ling there's the bell
Everybody's rushing and running to their lines.

Emily Wardle (9)
St Cuthbert's RC Primary School, Chester-Le-Street

WISH, WISH, WISH

I wish I didn't have to go to school
I wish I didn't feel pain
I wish I had my own swimming pool
I wish it would never rain!

I wish all my dreams would come true
I wish I could go and sit in the sky
I wish the world was blue
I wish I could fly

I wish there wasn't such a thing as night
I wish I could help the blind
I wish the sun wouldn't give off as much light
I wish everyone was kind

I wish I was never alone
I wish I knew everything
I wish grown-ups wouldn't moan
I wish I could sing

I wish there was an easy way out
I wish I was a hero
I wish a girl could be a scout
I wish I wasn't classed as a zero.

Laura Middleton (9)
St Cuthbert's RC Primary School, Chester-Le-Street

AT THE ZOO

Crocodiles' jaws snap,
Seals' fins clap.
Splash, splosh, splish,
Go the fish.
Kangaroos bounce,
Tigers pounce,
Lions roar
At their cage door.

People talking,
As they're walking,
Babies crying,
Dolphins diving.
Birds cheeping,
Cars beeping,
People crunching,
Giraffes munching
And me daydreaming.

Anne-Marie McLeman (9)
St Cuthbert's RC Primary School, Chester-Le-Street

THE PLAYGROUND

Before school, little children crying
Parents sighing
Pupils running about
Having a little shout
Ring, ring, the bell has gone
During school, parents talking
Birds squawking
Delivery vans beeping
The ground seeping.

Rebecca Graham (9)
St Cuthbert's RC Primary School, Chester-Le-Street

THE PLAYGROUND

Mr Lish is putting out the bins
While children are giggling
Parents are chattering
While babies' rattles are rattling
Children are dressed up neat
The parents are sitting on a seat
The bell rings so everyone lines up for school.

Amy E Murtha (9)
St Cuthbert's RC Primary School, Chester-Le-Street

THE PLAYGROUND

Children bouncing balls, *thump, thump, thump*
Mr Lish puts the bins out, *bump, bump, bump*
Children stamping their feet, *stamp, stamp, stamp*
Parents chatting to their friends, chat, chat, chat
The bell has rung
Time to come in.

Mark John Shead (9)
St Cuthbert's RC Primary School, Chester-Le-Street

THE PLAYGROUND

Mr Lish is putting out the bins, *clitter, clatter!*
Hannah is playing with me and Kate, *gas, gab!*
Faye is crying for Hannah, waa! Waa! Waa!
The birds are squawking over a worm, *squawk, squawk.*
Kate's mum is chatting to my mum, *chat, chat, chat!*

Jane Gibbon (9)
St Cuthbert's RC Primary School, Chester-Le-Street

WISH, WISH, WISH

I wish I could run as fast as Maurice Green
I wish I could score a goal
I wish I was seventeen
I wish I was a mole

I wish I could go to a football pitch
I wish I had a pet dog
I wish I could catch the golden Snitch
I wish I was smaller than a log

I wish I was cool as cool
I wish I was a rat
I wish I had a brilliant pool
I wish I had a nice cricket bat

I wish I was the size of a pin
I wish I could do an overhead flip
I wish, I wish, I was a biscuit tin
I wish my car was as big as a skip

I wish I was like Batman
I wish I was a bear
I wish I had a nice brown tan
I wish I had very short hair.

Jonathan Elder (9)
St Cuthbert's RC Primary School, Chester-Le-Street

THE PLAYGROUND

As Mr Lish puts out the bins
Listen, the rubbish is clattering
The children are playing tig
After 5 minutes, they start to pant

The parents are talking
The birds are squawking
All of a sudden, the bell rings, ding-dong
Then the children rush to their line.

Bernadette Hardman (9)
St Cuthbert's RC Primary School, Chester-Le-Street

WISH, WISH, WISH

I wish I had a kitten
I wish it could go out to play
I wish it played with a mitten
I wish it was a nice day

I wish it wouldn't snow
I wish the weather wasn't bad
I wish the snow would go
I wish I wasn't so sad

I wish I had a floppy toy
I wish it's colouring was brown
I wish its name was Floppy Roy
I wish it wore a gown

I wish my bag wasn't so full
I wish my bag was light
I wish my bag wasn't so dull
I wish it didn't give me a fright

I wish my friend could stay with me
I wish my friend could play
I wish my friend had tea today
I wish her name was Kay.

Francesca Citrone (8)
St Cuthbert's RC Primary School, Chester-Le-Street

WISH, WISH, WISH

I wish my mum would buy new clothes
I wish it was not raining
I wish I did not have to wear dicky bows
I wish I did not do training

I wish I was a football star
I wish I was tough
I wish I could get a car
I wish I was not allergic to fluff

I wish I was cool
I wish I had a tree house
I wish I had a pool
I wish I had a pet mouse

I wish I had lots of toys
I wish I had a blue chair
I wish all the people in my class were boys
I wish my Christmas tree was the shape of a bear

I wish I had hands of steel
I wish I had lots of gold
I wish I had a potter's wheel
I wish my writing was not bold.

Michael O'Brien (8)
St Cuthbert's RC Primary School, Chester-Le-Street

IN THE PLAYGROUND

Children playing, laughing, shouting
Parents chatting, watching babies gurgling
Crunch, crunch, rustle, rustle leaves
Splashing around

Screech, screech, squeak, squeak, cars parking
Ding-dong, the bell rings
Children sigh
Parents ask why.

Jennifer Mackay (9)
St Cuthbert's RC Primary School, Chester-Le-Street

WISH, WISH, WISH

I wish I didn't have an unpopular name
I wish I could skip
I wish I could play a game
I wish I didn't put on a stupid lip

I wish I was like other girls
I wish I was nice
I wish I had bouncy curls
I wish I could eat spice

I wish I looked good
I wish I felt great
I wish I wasn't fat with pud
I wish I wasn't too late

I wish my face would go nice and pretty
I wish I looked all right
I wish I didn't act so flitty
I wish I tried with all my might

I wish my dog had straight paws
I wish I had straight feet
I wish I didn't break my laws
I wish my skirt didn't have a pleat.

Rebecca Crossling (8)
St Cuthbert's RC Primary School, Chester-Le-Street

WISH, WISH, WISH

I wish it would snow.
I wish the weather wasn't so bad.
I wish the rain would go.
I wish I wasn't sad.

I wish I wouldn't bounce when I'm glad.
I wish everything was great.
I wish I wasn't so sad.
I wish . . . but wait, is that a snowflake?

I wish we could go on holiday.
I wish if we went, there was a lot of sun.
I wish on holiday we could stay.
I wish we could have a lot of fun.

I wish we could put up the Christmas tree.
I wish we were doing a Christmas play.
I wish the person to put on the tree decorations was me.
I wish my friend would come to stay.

I wish I could wear flowers in my hair.
I wish I had a toy Bagpuss.
I wish I could go to the fair.
I wish my mum didn't make such a fuss.

Francesca McLoughlin (8)
St Cuthbert's RC Primary School, Chester-Le-Street

THE PLAYGROUND

Before school starts, the birds are singing happily,
People are running, laughing and shouting,
The parents are chit, chit chatting,
Mr Lish puts out the bins, they make a racket, *clang, clang, cling,*

Ding, ding, there's the bell,
Time for school, children say bye to their parents
And give kisses and cuddles,
Then they go to their lines.

Hannah Anderson (9)
St Cuthbert's RC Primary School, Chester-Le-Street

WISH, WISH, WISH

I wish I was special.
I wish I was cool.
I wish I was as special as a petal.
I wish I was good at pool.

I wish I was smart.
I wish I was funky.
I wish I was good at art.
I wish I didn't look like a monkey.

I wish I had a snack.
I wish I was cool.
I wish I won the race.
I wish I wasn't a fool.

I wish I didn't go to school.
I wish I was clever.
I wish I was swimming in the pool.
I wish I had lots of leather.

I wish I had lots of mates.
I wish I didn't shake.
I wish I could stay up late.
I wish I didn't make mistakes.

Helen Curry (9)
St Cuthbert's RC Primary School, Chester-Le-Street

THE PLAYGROUND

The children start shouting to each other,
Then the birds start chirping,
Next I hear the people splashing in the puddles.
But now it gets louder and louder in the playground
And then I hear the bell ringing and ringing,
So everyone runs into their lines.

Matthew Waldock (9)
St Cuthbert's RC Primary School, Chester-Le-Street

THE UNIVERSE

Zipping through the universe,
Like a meteorite,
Stars and planets pass me by,
In the dead of night.

Zooming through a galaxy,
Millions of stars,
Full power, straight ahead,
To the planet Mars.

I think we took a wrong turn,
We're going round and round,
Maybe it's a black hole,
I think that's what we've found.

It's time to go back home again
Why does it have to be?
I better get there quickly though,
Or else I'll miss my tea.

Alexandra Tomlinson (11)
St Patrick's Primary School, Workington

MY SISTER

My sister gets on my nerves,
She hits me on the head.

My sister Emma is always in a mood,
She always takes it out on me.

She goes in her room,
When I go in, the door goes *boom!*

She doesn't like motorbikes,
She likes to have late nights.

My sister has a computer,
I have a PlayStation.

We don't always fight,
But she does get on my nerves!

John Paul Murray (11)
St Patrick's Primary School, Workington

FOOTBALL ATTACK!

When Gerrard scores,
The crowd roars.
When Riise tackles Rivaldo,
He's as bad as Ronaldo.

When Dudek is in the nets,
He's as good as he gets.
When Murphy is in midfield,
He's the best on the field.

Sam Smith (8)
St Patrick's Primary School, Workington

MY DOLPHIN

My little dolphin is called Debbie
She likes to play with her burst ball
She doesn't stop playing until she can't play anymore

My Debbie feels like rubber
But don't rub her out
You can tell when my Debbie's around
Her skin sparkles like the sun

Debbie likes eating a cod
But instead of eating
She plays with her food
Just like a child with a yoghurt.

Rachael McKenna (10)
St Patrick's Primary School, Workington

MY WORLD

Riding through the galaxy,
Skimming past the stars.
Surfing through the Milky Way,
Whizzing right past Mars!

Queen of the universe,
Princess of the moon.
Ruler of Cadbury's World,
Say no more to doom!

Soaring through space,
With no end to my glee -
This is *my* world,
So perfect - all for me!

Sophia McCrea (10)
St Patrick's Primary School, Workington

MY PETS

My pet pig's name is Paul,
He likes wandering in my hall.
All day long he eats his swill,
His home is a sty on a hill.

My pet pussy's name is Flip,
He dances to music and is really hip,
He sleeps all day in his bed,
His best friend is called Fred.

Percy is my pet parrot,
His favourite food is carrot.
He is dumb and can't talk,
Every now and again, he does squawk.

Nicholas Donohoe (11)
St Patrick's Primary School, Workington

MY DOG!

He's my dog
He's not a pup,
His name is Ben
And he loves to pick things up

He's black and white
With a funny old tail,
But in the morning,
Never fetches your mail.

But he still gets his biscuits
And he still gets his tea,
I still like to play with him,
When he jumps on me!

Rachel McKeating (10)
St Patrick's Primary School, Workington

MY BROTHERS!

My brothers aren't very nice,
They play boring games
That I don't like.

I wish they didn't,
Because they leave me out,
They're always around,
Somewhere about.

My little brother Liam,
Sometimes gets annoying,
When you kick him, he always starts crying,
My twin brother Ashley,
Kicks my brother Liam
And Liam is two years younger than him,
I can't imagine who he'll kick in the St Joseph's gym!

Jenny Ryan (10)
St Patrick's Primary School, Workington

WOLF

The wolf comes out at night
Howling in the moonlight
He goes hunting for food
To take back to his cubs
When they see him they run
To get there first
They fight and nip to get
The meat then they all
Scrabble to get some milk
Mother is waiting in the lair.

Kieran Blacklock (10)
St Patrick's Primary School, Workington

I HATE SCHOOL

Kick the tables,
Kick the chairs,
Kick the teacher down the stairs
And if it doesn't work,
Try again

The school dinners are so gross
And if the starters don't get you, the afters will,
Mouldy pudding and lumpy custard.

Lessons,
Well, you don't want to know,
They're not very good,
From my point of view,
But hey, *I hate school!*

Richard Poole (10)
St Patrick's Primary School, Workington

MY LITTLE SISTER

My little sister
You'd think she's really cute
But when you get to know her
You'll soon give her the boot

My mum wants to move
But when we go to see a house
She's the opposite of quiet as a mouse

I suppose she is quite cute
But when she was born
She got all the loot!

Daniel Little (10)
St Patrick's Primary School, Workington

MY BROTHERS

My brothers
Aren't like any others,
They are so mean
And like Mr Bean.
They don't like their clothes,
All they like to do is pose.
I think they pretend
To have a girlfriend.
Jonathan likes to play cards,
While Mark plays charades.
They like to drive cars,
I think they belong on Mars,
But I love them both the same.

Rebecca Dodgson (11)
St Patrick's Primary School, Workington

MY KITTEN

I've got a kitten
That likes sitting
On the sofa bed
She rolls around
Until she's found
With a dizzy head

Her name is Sammie
She cries for Mammy
She adores drinking milk
Her coat is like silk
She is the colour grey
And loves to sleep all day.

Kerry Browne (11)
St Patrick's Primary School, Workington

MY BROTHER

My brother is called Cameron
He likes the song Camellion
He really likes his bed
Except when he bangs his head
He always shouts for Mammy
But never shouts for Daddy
He's never liked a cockroach
But likes to go on a coach
He likes trains
Along with cranes
He likes my dog
But cries in the fog
He likes his teddy bear
But he knows we don't care
That is my brother, Cameron.

Brett Chicken (10)
St Patrick's Primary School, Workington

AUTUMN!

When autumn comes
The leaves fall down
Orange, red, yellow, green and brown
They all scatter at my feet
When people put them in a pile
They look so neat
All over the pavement
When you look down
Some people would put on a frown
So when autumn comes, get out and play
And you will see the leaves each day
When autumn comes.

Emma McDowell (11)
St Patrick's Primary School, Workington

A Day At Golf

Golf is great
You can play with a mate
I came to the course in a car
And on the first hole, I got a par

I somehow got an albatross
When I saw a man slip on some moss
You need to play very well
If you don't want to be locked in a cell

Tiger Woods is very good
Even when he is stuck in mud
People go to the driving range
But it will never change

People can get a hole in one
Especially people called Don
I like playing this game
Some people might think the same.

Matthew Hoban (9)
St Patrick's Primary School, Workington

Swimming

Swimming, swimming
Butterfly, back, breast and front crawl,
Front crawl is my favourite
And my fastest.

Galas, galas are really great,
But it's the travelling I really hate,
Trophies and medals I'd like to achieve,
As long as I try my best, I don't mind.

Time trials are really easy,
But I prefer to swim.
You race against the clock
And achieve your time.

Sammie Kirkbride (10)
St Patrick's Primary School, Workington

MONSTERS, WITCHES AND GIANTS

They creep up at night,
As soon as you see them, you're in for a fright.

Trying to ignore them horrible things,
The guitar-playing giant just sings and sings.

Try to hide down in the basement,
Then you find a great amazement.

Monsters, witches and giants,
Could pop out of anywhere,
Monsters, witches and giants,
They really would give you a scare.

Here comes the giant,
He stands in your garden,
Then he *burps*,
Oops, pardon.

The hairy cyclops,
Plays with the Sindy
And howls away,
When it gets windy.

You'd better keep out of their way,
Or you're in for a painful day.

John Hall (10)
St Patrick's Primary School, Workington

MY CRAZY CATS

I've got two cats
People think they're brats
Diving under the sofa
Running everywhere

I've got two cats
They're crazy in every way
One thing they can really do is play

I've got two cats
They're called Oscar and Molly
They love to play with my cousin's dolly
They whine all day to get some food
And they always end up in a mood.

Emma Norris (11)
St Patrick's Primary School, Workington

THERE'S ALWAYS A BIGGER FISH

There once was a goldfish
That lived quite happily,
But another fish came
And ate it up for tea.

The next fish waited
Until the sea was dark,
Planned its next attack
And was eaten by a shark.

This shark waited
For the stars of God,
Then swam out
Into a fisherman's rod.

Ashley Ryan (10)
St Patrick's Primary School, Workington

MY BEST FRIEND

My best friend has fair blonde hair,
My best friend has small blue eyes,
You will have a true kind friend
If you could have my best friend.

My best friend makes me feel
As if I were head over heels,
My best friend has glasses too
But I don't care, she's my best friend.

My best friend will care for me,
My best friend will share with me,
Me and my best friend have fun,
She's my best friend, that I know.

My best friend is Kate.

Rebecca Scott (11)
St Patrick's Primary School, Workington

SMELLY MELLY

There was a girl called Melly
Whose feet were rather smelly
She scrubbed them so hard
With a big block of lard
Now they look
Like a big pile of jelly
She walked down the street
With her smelly boyfriend Pete
She went in the shop
The men and women said, 'Ough!'
It must be smelly Melly.

Sam Ruddy (8)
St Patrick's Primary School, Workington

STORM

S   o strong against the hurricane
T   hunder crossing the blackest mane
O   range eyes, sparkling, glistening
R   oaming wild, ears listening
M   ist surrounds the smooth black body
      chewing sugarcane

H   ooves pounding against the ground
O   r a swish of a tail that makes no sound
R   unning against the wind and rain
S   teadily cantering, the beat - the same
E   lectric Storm is her name
      lightning is her game.

Jenna Hall (11)
St Patrick's Primary School, Workington

FOOTBALL MAD

F   ans of Liverpool are the best,
O   wen plays up front and scores lots of goals,
O   h Owen is the best!
T   he team is absolutely fabulous,
B   erger is a great player, he's my favourite.
A   ll of Manchester United are rubbish,
L   ots of teams are good, but not as good as Liverpool.
L   eeds are show-offs, they all tackle too hard.

M   um doesn't like football,
A   untie doesn't either,
D   ad watches it all the time!

Jake Smith (8)
St Patrick's Primary School, Workington

BEST FRIENDS FOREVER!

B eing Katie Baker's best friend is great
E veryone says we're No 1 mates
S haring things, having fun
T rue best friends, always together!

F unny, caring, always sharing
R unning, jumping, never tired
I n bad situations, she helps me out
E veryone, anything would tell you
N ever arguing or shouting at each other
D oing everything together
S leeping at each other's houses

F riends together, never nasty
O utings we enjoy going on
R ound and round the clock we play
E veryone says we are
V ery, very close
E verything goes away when we play
R ich or poor, we will always be together!

Jade Cunningham (10)
St Patrick's Primary School, Workington

MY FAMILY

F orgiving and forgetting
A nimals love you
M ums and dads are always there to help you through good and bad
I love my family
L ove is always there when you need it
Y ou should always remember your family wherever you are.

Leanne Hoban (9)
St Patrick's Primary School, Workington

My Birthday

My favourite day of the year
Is, of course, you're right
My brother will always fear
My

B   esides all the presents
I   t's so much fun
R   ollerblading at my party
T   wice I will fall
H   aving lots of fun
D   ancing at my disco
A   round the dance floor
Y   ear in and year out
     My favourite day of course is
     My birthday!

Kate Chorley (11)
St Patrick's Primary School, Workington

My Friend, Carrie

C   ool
A   mazing
R   ough
R   eally great
I   ncredible
E   xciting

My friend Carrie is the best,
She is better than the rest!

Simone Wilson (8)
St Patrick's Primary School, Workington

ANIMALS

Some animals are small
And some animals are tall
Some animals are scary
And some animals are hairy

A snake is long and scary
But isn't the slightest bit hairy
A tiger is big and has stripes of black
But the rest of its body is like an orange sack
A gorilla is big and is quite fat
I would say, it's ten times a cat
An adult giraffe is incredibly tall
Probably taller than our school hall
A big rhinoceros has a great horn
If I can remember, they eat grass and corn
I like animals, where would I be
If I never had them to see?

Martyn Wood (10)
St Patrick's Primary School, Workington

MY SCHOOL

S   chool is always fun,
C   ool is what school is.
H   omework is what we get,
O   ut in the cold we play.
O   pen from Monday to Friday,
L   ate is when we get home from school.

Catherine Steel (9)
St Patrick's Primary School, Workington

FLOPSEY, MY PET

F rom the day I got my rabbit, she was funny,
L ovely, cool and sometimes round the bend.
O ur friendship will never end.
P laying tiggy and hide-and-seek.
S he likes the song by Mis-teeq,
E very day finding something new.
Y ou would love her if you saw her too.

M aybe she is a bit silly,
Y esterday she scared my pigeon, Milly.

P eople laugh at her,
E njoying her tricks,
T rue friendship, even though we are a different mix.

Emily Grima (9)
St Patrick's Primary School, Workington

BEST FRIENDS

B est friends are there for you,
E veryone needs one too.
S pecial in every way,
T reat you nicely every day.

F alling out with your friend,
R eady to make friends in the end.
I like having a best friend,
E very one of them shares a trend.
N ow I just can't wait,
D ay and night till I see my mate,
S o that's how friendship is!

Kerry Hall (10)
St Patrick's Primary School, Workington

MY BEST FRIEND

M y best friend is Leanne
Y ou might like one too

B eginning a friendship that never ends
E verything you do together you will always remember
S pecial people in your lives
T ogether forever

F orgiving and forgetting
R ough times but you get through them
I f you need anybody, they're always there
E verybody needs one
N ever-ending friendship
D on't ever go without them.

Laura Skilling (10)
St Patrick's Primary School, Workington

RAINDROPS

R aindrops fall to the ground
A s they make a tiny sound
I n holes they make puddles
N esting birds wake up by dribbles
D own the rain trickles
R ound the whole world
O ut through the garden
P itter-patter down the street
S ilently splashing the people it meets.

Carrie Hall (8)
St Patrick's Primary School, Workington

DRAGONS

Dragons can be big and small
And very, very tall.
They have scaly skin
And can do the best spin.
Dragons can breathe fire,
They are the quickest flier.

Dragons have sharp claws
And enormous jaws.
They ram into things with rage
And can smash out of any type of cage.
Their wings are strong
And their tails are very, very long.
If you meet them, they'll eat you alive,
Then no one will survive.

Stuart Quinn (10)
St Patrick's Primary School, Workington

ARNIE IS MY DOG

Arnie is a good boy
He loves to play with his toy
Then his best friend Bess comes to play
Bess always makes his day
Arnie is as black as night
But his eyes are very bright
When he licks me his tongue is wet
It's as wet as it can get
Arnie is clever and smart
Dear Arnie belongs in my heart.

Jessica Taylor (8)
St Patrick's Primary School, Workington

MY FAMILY

My family are all very loyal,
We all like digging in the garden soil.
My mum, my dad and Richard too,
Are all too old to go to the zoo.

My mum is loving and caring
And all the new fashion trends she's wearing,
My dad is always on the go,
But he takes me to the local show.

Richard is football mad,
Although he is a clever lad.

I love them all, no matter what,
Even though they are a fussy lot.
I don't care,
Because they are mine, so there!

Lucy Hoban (10)
St Patrick's Primary School, Workington

SKATEBOARDING

When I skate I'm always late,
The boys in the park laugh at me,
When I get the wrong date,
I don't care, I'll knock for my mate
And we will skate, skate, skate!

Skateboarding is the best,
I scare the birds out of their nest,
All the people stare at me,
When I skate along and smile with glee!

Stuart McCullock (8)
St Patrick's Primary School, Workington

CRICKET IS FUN

Cricket is fun
You usually play it in the sun
The players are dressed in white
They hit the ball with all their might
They might hit a six or maybe a four
Then you will hear the crowd roar

I play cricket in the park
And I stay out until it's dark
Cricket is an enjoyable game
Lots of players have experienced fame.

Callum Doyle (8)
St Patrick's Primary School, Workington

KNIGHTS

There was a knight,
His armour was too tight.
All day long he stood in mud,
Surrounded by dark forest and wood.
One day a villain came,
Galloping along the lane,
He took one look at the knight
And ran off in a fright!

Scott Auty (9)
St Patrick's Primary School, Workington

SUPER BOWL

American football is the best
I like it better than the rest
When someone scores
They give them a round of applause

When McNabb passes the ball
All the crowd starts to call
The Super Bowl is a big tournament
The players give it a hundred percent.

Tommy Wilson (8)
St Patrick's Primary School, Workington

SPEEDWAY

Speedway is good,
They ride on mud,
I think Stoney is the best,
Better than all the rest,
He is fast
And never the last,
They go four times round the track,
If they break the tapes they have to go back.

Stacey Johnston (8)
St Patrick's Primary School, Workington

LIONS, LIONS, LIONS

Lions creep in the forest
Lions are very modest
Lions live in a pride
Lions like to hide

Lions are brill
Lions like to chill
Lions are simply the best
Better than all the rest!

Megan Ranson (9)
St Patrick's Primary School, Workington

SMELLY KELLY

Smelly Kelly bought some jelly
Because she wanted to fill her belly.
Her mother was mad,
Kelly was sad,
Her friend was tall,
But she was very small.

One day she went to town,
In her pink dressing gown,
She walked down the street
And bumped into Pete,
He asked for some jelly,
She said, 'Sorry, it's all in my belly.'

Robert Little (8)
St Patrick's Primary School, Workington

MY CAT FELIX

My cat is getting quite fat,
He sits and dreams on his mat.

He jumps on my bed
And makes me bang my head.

He doesn't like the rain,
He always uses his brain.

He jumps at my mum for his tea
And he likes my middle name, Lee.

I love my cat where would I be
Without him beside me?

Nicholas Wood (9)
St Patrick's Primary School, Workington

WINTER

I've always liked winter, especially when it snows,
Grab your sledge and go down the hills.

Snowballs get thrown in your hair,
It rains and it hailstones, but is never fair,
Kids enjoy sliding everywhere.

Dean Norris (8)
St Patrick's Primary School, Workington

MY MAD WORLD

The moon is a big white marble
The sun is a huge big star
The Earth is going up and down
This place is going bizarre

The streams, a big flow of lemonade
The trees are made of broccoli
The muddy banks are chocolate
And our crisps are always soggy

Our dogs live in a fish tank
A tortoise has a lion's legs
And whales have shrunk to the size of a tiny peg

The grass has turned purple
The leaves have turned red
The birds have turned yellow
And they peck your head.

Josh Adamson (10)
Shotton Hall Junior School, Peterlee

MY CRAGSIDE IMPRESSIONS

The kitchen was way ahead of its time,
Dining room to wine and dine!
The yellow bedroom, oh how bright,
The house was full of hydro light!
Cragside house, lots to see,
The morning room for your cup of tea!
The boudoir for the ladies only,
Wouldn't Lord Armstrong get quite lonely?
The drawing room with a huge fireplace,
The gallery with lots of space!
The scullery, how dull and cold,
The red bedroom, the colour very bold!
The bath suite used to be very hot,
The study, Lord Armstrong used quite a lot,
People would visit to come and see,
This wonderful house deep in the country!

Ruth French (10)
Shotton Hall Junior School, Peterlee

FEELINGS

Helpful is helping your mum when she is bad,
Happy is Christmas presents,
Sad is losing a pet,
Miserable is getting no pocket money,
Angry is a teacher telling people off,
Surprise is when you open presents,
Fear is a big venomous snake,
Joy is seeing relatives from Australia,
Confusion is my sister telling jokes.

Dean Collings (11)
Shotton Hall Junior School, Peterlee

BURGLARS

What should we nick next?
I know, maybe the TV because I want to watch Teletext.
Let's get the money jar,
Do you think they have a bar?
Let's look for a purse,
What if we're under a curse?
What if I get the microwave
Or maybe the micro scooter?
Let's get the dog
Or the fake frog.
Do you want to go and get the watch
Or what about the torch?
I'll go and get the key,
But what about me?
Let's go and get some wings,
I think we should stop being burglars and nicking things.

Holly Venners (10)
Shotton Hall Junior School, Peterlee

FEELING . . .

Happy is white chocolate,
Sad is when it's raining,
Confusion in English,
Helpful is helping someone,
Fear is war and suffering,
Cold is outside in the rain,
Amazement is science,
Kindness is giving people things,
Weirdness is how many things we have not seen.

Jordan Wilson (11)
Shotton Hall Junior School, Peterlee

I Am, That Is

I fought off the mighty cats, bare-pawed,
They lost so they went off and roared
I am, that is

I never turned and ran, but stayed
And lashed out with my mighty sword
I fought and fought and fought
Till they ran, that villainous hoard
I am, that is

'Twas two winter's ago, I fought a battle in the snow
I beat the hoard, but got injured outside
Redwall, they took me into Great Hall
I am, that is
Beware.

Mathew Geldard (9)
Shotton Hall Junior School, Peterlee

Dragons

Dragons flying.
Dragons are fierce.
Dragons breathing fire.
A dragon roaring in pain.
Dragons good and bad.
Dragons are mythological creatures.
Dragons retreating because they are not numbered.
I wonder what the world would be like
If dragons were real?

Stuart Robinson (11)
Shotton Hall Junior School, Peterlee

DRAGONS

Some dragons are red
Some dragons are green
Few are blue
Most are mean

Some dragons are scary
Some dragons are kind
Some dragons are ugly
Some are hard to find

Some dragons have wings
Some dragons breathe fire
Some dragons are queens and kings.

Claire Barrass (10)
Shotton Hall Junior School, Peterlee

CHRISTMAS

Christmas lunch
A drink of punch
Christmas cards
Laughing hearts

Snowmen building
Choirs singing
Christmas turkeys
Lots of parties

Nativity plays
Turkey trays
Christmas Day
It's a fun day.

Hannah Pearson (10)
Shotton Hall Junior School, Peterlee

CHRISTMAS MORNING

On the morning of Christmas Day,
It seemed like a day in May.
I woke up at half-past seven
And I went to bed at eleven.
I ran downstairs to see what I had
And my mum and dad, they went mad.
I took off the paper and opened the box
And inside the box was a pair of socks.
But the biggest present of all,
Was at least four foot tall.
My mouth did then drop,
I started to hop.
In excitement and joy,
I was shouting, 'Oh boy!'
It was the biggest teddy I'd ever seen,
My sister and I were very keen
And that was my morning of Christmas Day,
I'd tell you the tale of my Christmas lunch,
But right now, I need to munch.

Glyn Pallister (10)
Shotton Hall Junior School, Peterlee

DRAGONS

Did you know dragons don't exist?
People believe they did - long ago.
But what about St George and the dragon?
Did he ever see one? - We'll never know!

Dragons are different in colour and size,
People believe they are huge and green.
How do people know these things?
Because a dragon has never been seen!

Not all dragons are evil and fierce,
Some folk believe they are gentle and tame
And others think dragons all look different,
Yet others think they're all the same!

Dragons appear in stories alone,
They may be animals but they're not real!
If dragons were alive, would they talk?
If dragons were alive, would they feel?

Hayley Groves (10)
Shotton Hall Junior School, Peterlee

SCHOOL DAYS

Nine in the morning, we go to school,
Some find it bad, some find it cool.
Morning break falls, we all celebrate,
We all hang around, so we will be late.
Afternoon comes, hip hip hooray,
It's getting close to the end of the day.

Our lunch is a school dinner, some say it's yuck,
But I think if you have one, you are in luck.
You can also have a packed lunch, bring it from home,
Sandwich, pasty, even a scone.
Lunchtime over, more lessons, *great!*
Sometimes it's a subject you *really* hate!

Home time comes, time for tea,
Going home, maybe a shopping spree.
Parents waiting at the gate,
We're always dawdling, we're always late.
Looking forward to the weekend ahead,
But we have to do our homework instead!

Michelle Clark (10)
Shotton Hall Junior School, Peterlee

LIGHT IS . . .

Fire with burning flames of light,
The brightness of the moon at night!
Lightning flashing on the ground,
Faster than the speed of sound!
Fireworks banging in the sky,
Stars shooting, flying by!

Rainbows showing off their colours!

Candlelight we need at night,
Sun setting out of sight!
Sparks of light zooming past,
Electricity getting really fast!
Flares flying all around,
Flashing up from the ground!

Colours as bright as they can be!

Michelle Fullard (11)
Shotton Hall Junior School, Peterlee

THE CREATURE

As I lay on the hillside and looked above,
I could see something flying high in the air,
It had a long scaly neck and glaring eyes,
You could see if it played with you, it wouldn't play fair,
Huge round nostrils with smoke creeping out,
A massive round body all colours of the rainbow,
Would stand out a mile away, north, south, east or west,
If its favourite food is birds, it would never catch a crow.
It has a tail so long, you wouldn't believe it,
I wonder if I'll ever see this weird creature again.

Kelsey Douglas (10)
Shotton Hall Junior School, Peterlee

ALIEN

I met an alien the other day,
He was weird in every way,
He had 55 hands and 55 toes,
As well as one big long nose.
He had a strange wooden leg
And a wooden toe made from a peg.
He had 80 ears and 80 eyes
And was followed by 40 flies.
He had hair all over the place,
Which I thought was a big disgrace.
He said he's once been to Mars,
But had never even heard of stars.
When I suggested we phoned his mum,
He replied, 'She was no fun.'
Just when I worried he'd stay here,
In a puff of smoke he did disappear.

Jessica Errington (10)
Shotton Hall Junior School, Peterlee

LIGHT IS . . .

Fireworks, burning and flashing,
Lightning, striking and crashing.
The sun beaming down on the ground,
A light from the lighthouse signalling ships,
The stars that look as big as pencil tips.
Electricity flowing around the house,
Candles burning as bright as a torch,
You could even put them in your porch.
The flames of a fire sparkling bright,
Like a solar beam in the night!

Laura Talbot (10)
Shotton Hall Junior School, Peterlee

CHRISTMAS MORNING

I run down the stairs, that are really soft,
I look straight ahead, Santa's been from the loft,
I see all the presents that look really good,
I can't wait to have the Christmas pud.
I wonder what I'll get? I'll have to see,
Is all this great stuff really for me?
I can't wait to use my new telescope,
My mum will love her new smelling soap.
I shout for my dad, but he's shaving his beard,
He's got one like Santa, that's just what I feared!
All these great toys were just for me,
The teddy, the doll and the bumblebee.
I go in the kitchen to get something to eat,
Then I see something rubbing against my feet,
It's the cutest kitten I've ever seen,
But I wonder where he's been?

Carly Fishwick (10)
Shotton Hall Junior School, Peterlee

DREAMING

When I am dreaming,
I go into a misty land,
Where someone mysterious takes my hand,
Higher and higher, up, up we go,
No more worries, nowhere to go,
Floating along through the clouds,
So many familiar places, so many sounds.

Kate Gibson (9)
Shotton Hall Junior School, Peterlee

MERMAID

Mermaid, mermaid, swimming by the sea,
Why don't you come out and play with me?
Mermaid, mermaid, swimming by the sea,
Please come out 'cause I would not hurt thee.
Mermaid, mermaid, swimming by the sea,
Come out and put a dress on just for me.
Mermaid, mermaid, swimming by the sea,
Would you like to try a cup of tea?
Mermaid, mermaid, swimming by the sea,
Do you have a brother called Lee?
Mermaid, mermaid, swimming by the sea,
Why don't you come out and play with me?

Sophie Coldwell (9)
Shotton Hall Junior School, Peterlee

HAIKUS

Snowman, body roll.
  Snowballs coming, run, chuck back.
    Snow cold, need gloves, quick.

Suntan, burning, cream.
  Swim, lovely sea, warm water.
    Sandcastles being squashed.

School, science is good.
  Dinnertime, yummy, love food.
    Lesson time, wonder!

Craig Benton (11)
Shotton Hall Junior School, Peterlee

WAY OUT IN SPACE

Way out in space,
So far away,
Hiding in the clouds.
Jupiter so purple,
It's so big and round,
I wish that I could see it.
All of the rest as well,
Neptune, Uranus, Pluto,
So many, it's hard to tell.
Maybe there is life in space,
Aliens of all kinds,
Nobody really knows the truth,
They'll be very hard to find.
Nine planets all together,
Some with rings around,
I hope I get to look in space,
Just a little peep!

Fallon Hickman (11)
Shotton Hall Junior School, Peterlee

FEELINGS . . .

Happiness is Ibiza.
Fear is an infection!
Surprised is a limo!
Kindness is making dinner.
Strangeness is the light going off!
Surprised is your tent falling down.
Jealousy is when your brother gets more pocket money.
Happiness is a holiday!

Harley Ferguson (10)
Shotton Hall Junior School, Peterlee

SPACE IS...

Space is a huge dark place
With everything you want.

Thousands and millions of stars
Not forgetting the planets, Jupiter, Venus and Mars.

Space is a quiet place
Because nothing ever talks.

But then again, I might be wrong
Because people say that things walk.

Space is a dangerous place
With asteroids flying all over.

It's a very good thing that Earth is protected
Or we would *suffer!*

Annabelle Edwards (10)
Shotton Hall Junior School, Peterlee

SPACE COULD BE...

Space could be a dangerous place,
Pluto could be a very important case
And yet it could just be a place that doesn't
Need an important case,
Could it be a freezing place in space?
Nobody will ever know,
Everything in space just floats except for us,
We don't.

Michelle Keighley (10)
Shotton Hall Junior School, Peterlee

MY BABY BROTHER

I have a baby brother, Ryan is his name
He always laughs and giggles when I pull a funny face
He's just learned how to walk and he's learning how to talk

He eats his dinner and drinks his milk
And then he tries to pinch mine too
He likes to eat milk chocolate, but he gets it everywhere
On this clothes, around his face and even in his hair

He likes to watch the telly and dances to music too
He likes to play with his daddy - who throws him in the air
He tickles him all over until he quickly runs away

He loves his nightly bath time, when he plays with his tug boat
He likes to splish and splash and soak our mummy too
He likes to blow big bubbles and laughs when they go pop
And then when it is bedtime he goes into his cot
He's wrapped up warm and snugly and he sucks his thumb a lot
He is my baby brother and I love him lots and lots.

Andrew Bell (9)
Shotton Hall Junior School, Peterlee

MY DRAGON!

D   is for dangerous which my dragon is,
R   is for rage which my dragon can be in,
A   is for air which my dragon flies with,
G   is for generous which my dragon definitely is not,
O   is for open when my dragon escapes, and
N   is for nasty which my dragon is, a lot.

Helen Clynes (9)
Shotton Hall Junior School, Peterlee

WHATIF

(Based on 'Whatif' by Shel Silverstein)

While I lay down thinking here, what if there were whatifs in my ear,
Partying and prancing all night long, singing the same old whatif song.
Whatif I went to school and flunked the test?
Whatif green hairs grow on my chest?
Whatif someone puts poison in my cup?
Whatif I stop getting good luck?
Whatif nobody likes me?
Whatif I have a horrible tea?
Whatif the custard in school is all lumpy?
Whatif the mashed potato is all bumpy?
But is there anyone in this new school, just plain and normal just
like me? Please!

Francesca Edwards (10)
Shotton Hall Junior School, Peterlee

MY VOYAGE TO SPACE

I'm in space floating past lots of stars
Using rockets side by side as if they were cars
Don't look at the sun or you'll become blind!
Go the other direction for planets you'll find
You'll see Mercury, Venus and our beautiful planet too!
I'll keep the chat going on especially just for you
It's very exciting looking at the planets slowly orbiting the sun
It may be very slow but when you're there it's fun
Now I know why Russia and America had a race
Because it's very fascinating here in space.

Craig Rhodes (10)
Shotton Hall Junior School, Peterlee

THE GHYLL SCRAMBLE

The light coming in to show the trickling water
Like blood veins trickling in and out of rocks,
I fought nervously against the violent water.
We slipped against smooth, mossy rocks
Which felt like a face cloth lying on a stone,
Foaming, bubbling water like froth on the top of Coke,
Delicate ferns like spiders peeping through the water.
Rocks making it uncomfortable for you to climb,
Water gushing into my wellies as I tripped through mini waterfalls.
Rocks like mini footballs making you fall into the water,
Moss-like, green ladybirds sprawled across the rocks,
Big boulders like whales looking up at you.
We splashed clumsily past the boulders and rocks,
The ice-cold water making you feel like an ice cube.
Fallen trees blocking our way,
Tree roots like snakes coiling up,
I struggled cautiously up a grassy bank.
Then I stumbled through the tunnel under the road
Making my way past the rocks.
Then suddenly we *emerge* into light!

Claire Donald (9)
Skelton Primary School, Penrith

THE GHYLL CLIMB

Water passed by me gently as I stepped into the ghyll,
Sunlight flickered ahead,
Snake-like trees loomed out,
Frothing torrents passed me scuttering and stuttering,
Water snaked, twisting and turning past me, jumping over rocks.

Rocks, silky with lichen,
Rocks, jagged on cliffs,
Water fell past me in gushes tumbling and turning
As I climbed out of the ghyll,
It was like going back to the real world.

Gareth Hughes (9)
Skelton Primary School, Penrith

THE GHYLL SCRAMBLE

I scrambled down the mini cliff face that leered down at me,
The cold tingling water seeped into my submarine wellies,
Stumbling upstream against the current.
No time to stop and admire the green, luscious ferns.
Water snaked around rocks, slippery rocks,
Water tumbled into deep pools,
While spitting and hissing at me.
Objects took the easy way down,
Lying lazily on water while drifting downstream;
Further upstream, other objects rolled and foamed.
The water danced around me like a circus acrobat,
Jumping over the waterfall to smash onto the rocks.
Stumbling over slippery rocks,
Like the back of a hippo barring your way.
Crusty lichens cased the smooth, rounded rocks,
Trees reached out to grab you with twiggy fingers,
Ferns turned with the wind as if to watch me.
As I emerged from the gorge,
I came into civilisation and the real world.

Charlotte Miller (10)
Skelton Primary School, Penrith

THE GHYLL SCRAMBLE

Icy cold water slithers round warm legs
As I cautiously lift myself down into unknown waters.
I look upstream,
Great bold rocks peer at me like giant monsters,
All is quiet.
Nervously I start to stumble up the smooth rocks,
Cautiously scrambling along the cliff edge,
Clinging onto weak spiky ferns.
A miniature waterfall tumbles over the rocks,
Blindly I try to find a foothold in a mass of bubbly foam.
Finally I scramble up on top and plunge into still, glass water.
Precariously I edge my way across the tiny ledge.
Jump far out, jump further out and . . .
Splash!
A cold shiver runs up my back,
I'm pulled back to safety,
Reaching the top, great beams of sunlight dry my soaking body,
The blackness of the ghyll behind and the light of the world in front.

Amanda Jackson (10)
Skelton Primary School, Penrith

THE GHYLL

Cold icy water gushing past me,
Nervously waiting to start the long scramble,
Rocks hidden under clear water,
We climbed onwards, upwards happily, unaware of clusters of rocks,
Water trickling through rocks quickly.
Nervously climbing, touching spongy green moss,
Water getting darker, as bushy trees tower over.

Standing in front a barrier of tall boulders,
Scrambling over a barrier of tall boulders,
A pool of cold icy water lying there like a shiny, wooden floor,
Brave people plunging into icy water, others retreating,
Then climbing up slippery banks.
At last the sunlight beamed at me,
I looked down at the dark world beneath.

Kerry Donald (11)
Skelton Primary School, Penrith

THE GHYLL SCRAMBLE

It was freezing as my feet stepped in,
Water lapped over them,
Started running down my wellies!
Roots and branches curved round rocks and boulders,
Water gushed forcefully towards me,
I knew I had to climb something.
A mini waterfall, the water spraying at me,
Water all bubbly and frothy in a deep pool,
Climbing up the waterfall,
Up the black and grey rocks at the top,
Soggy green moss glowed in the sunlight,
Ferns tangled everywhere.
Under rocks,
Over branches,
I climbed the rocks boldly,
Water trickled down little paths like snakes
And finally I climbed into the open air.

Heather Blanshard (9)
Skelton Primary School, Penrith

THE GHYLL SCRAMBLE

The water racing around my feet, gushing and plunging over the rocks.
Twisting water everywhere making gurgly sounds,
Slipping over rocks with water filling my wellies.
Trees on both sides with twisting branches and waving leaves;
Rocks like animals - huge elephants and tiny pebble mice,
Sliding into pools of icy water, flooding me,
Rocks like helping hands carrying me up,
The gyrating water throwing itself around like it's alive,
Boldly climbing up the steep, grey rock face;
Angry and spluttering, flowing and sprawling water,
Lichen clinging to the rocks likes splodges of paint;
Pools silky smooth and waterfalls ending in a shower of foamy water,
Water playing, licking at the banks, stuttering to get past rocks.
Spindly trees growing towards the light and tall trees block any view
Of human life.
Moss like a springy, green mattress,
Slipping, sliding, twisting and gliding,
Water dancing across the rocks.
At the top, now climbing on the ledge, the pool below my feet,
Sparkling and still.
Then I plunge into the icy depths, the surface broken,
I swim to the rocks, walking through the trees,
The road ahead and the sun bearing down,
My wellies full of water, I walk back down the road,
Back to civilisation from the gloom of the lost valley.

Katie Hughes (11)
Skelton Primary School, Penrith

THE GHYLL SCRAMBLE

I hop into a fresh new world,
A harmless little ghyll,
With rocks dotted here and there
And shallow, smooth, clear water.
The rocks are smooth,
The ghyll is tight,
It's a wonderful, pleasant sight.

Now it's getting deeper,
It's fluttering, stuttering on,
Trees are on the large, steep banks,
With lots of kinds of leaves.
There are green leaves,
Brown leaves,
Red leaves,
Big leaves,
Small leaves
And oh, so many of them.

I'm now at the angry top of the ghyll,
It's getting more serious,
Over rocks,
Over falls,
Sometimes having to duck and crawl.
Then I scramble on and on,
Till I finally reach my safety,
At the tarmac of the busy main road
And out of my little ghyll world!

Freddie Stewart (10)
Skelton Primary School, Penrith

THE GHYLL SCRAMBLE

A smooth river with washed-up rocks sparkled in the sunlight,
Old gnarled trees and fresh, bright, new ones stood together on the
bank,
Ferns like a spider glimmered with raindrops,
Rocks speckled with lichen lay down below them,
The smooth river gained power,
More waterfalls ending in frothy bubbles and pools like glass,
Small cliff faces with overhanging moss above them
And then the biggest waterfall!
Water comes tumbling and stumbling over the edge
And then we climb out of the ghyll and onto the hard dry road.

Clemency Jolly (9)
Skelton Primary School, Penrith

STOLEN

They mug the rich and steal from the unwealthy,
Catnap the cats that they hate so much.

They are dirty bags of rotten bone stealing food,
They live in dirty barns from cast-out animals,
Who lived with the farmers.

Round the world they steal and nick,
Nobody can stop them, there are too many.
They mug the rich and steal from the unwealthy,
Beware! Or your pockets will feel empty!

Ben Shaw (10)
Storth CE Primary School, Milnthorpe

SCHWARZENEGGER'S SHOP TO TOWN

Arnold went to town
He went to town in a dressing gown
He got a present for his mum
By gum!
He went to a shop
And got a lamb chop
But it went missing like a flea
Oh where could it be?
Arnold looked here and there
He even searched a bear
But he couldn't find it
Not a bit!
He lost his hidden treasure
Still now, it is waiting to be found.

Jonathan Palmer (10)
Storth CE Primary School, Milnthorpe

MY FAMILY

My dad is surprisingly tall,
My mum is only small,
My brothers and my sisters are pests,
I just wish I could shove them in a nest,
My grandma isn't too bad,
But my grandad is worse than bad!
My house is very nice, but full of little mice,
My family is a horror,
I want to leave tomorrow.

Aaron Marrs (9)
Storth CE Primary School, Milnthorpe

HIDDEN TREASURES

H   is for 'Hmmm, I don't know!'
I   is for ice cream, too cold!
D   is for dragon, roooarrr!
D   is for danger, 'Danger, danger!'
E   is for easy, piece of cake,
N   is for 'No money! I'm hungry!'

T   is for tom cat, miaow!
R   is for 'Run!' 'What from?'
E   is for everybody sing, doh ra . . .
A   is for *aagghhh help!*
S   is for sausages, sizzle, sizzle,
U   is for 'You', 'No, me, me.'
R   is for ride, no it's my turn,
E   is for EastEnders, Ricky!
S   is for surfing, cool.

Thomas McGregor (10)
Storth CE Primary School, Milnthorpe

HIDDEN HORSES

I looked over the mountains
Then something stopped me
It was dazzling, it was a Welsh cob
The pony had white forelock and man-tail
It was pieball and big, I would think it was 13.2 hands high
But remember horses are great!
I love horses.

Jessica Shaw (8)
Storth CE Primary School, Milnthorpe

HIDDEN TREASURE

H idden treasure
I n the sand
D ig, dig
D ig
E veryone's
N early there

T reasure being lifted
R osie, Reanne and
E laine
A re helping
S and and roots are flying
U nderneath the sand
R osie, Reanne and
E laine, digging in the sand

O pening the lid
N early opened

A padlock on the box
N early knocked it off

I feel
S o happy
L ying on the beach
A treasure box comes up
N obody is
D igging now.

Sam Dutton (8)
Storth CE Primary School, Milnthorpe

ACROSTIC POEM

J umps like a cat on a hot tin roof
A ttacks like a silent leopard
C ooks like the Naked Chef
K icks like Bruce Lee
I n danger all the time
E ats like he has never eaten before

C heeky monkey!
H its like a kung fu expert
A nswers Anne Robinson's questions and gets them all wrong
N ever pays the chef.

James McGregor (9)
Storth CE Primary School, Milnthorpe

HIDDEN TREASURE

Hide the treasure and stash it away
Look at it another distant day
A precious letter from someone far away
It could be a book or a teddy bear
This fragile thing needs a lot of care
Look out if you dare!

It could be in a casket, a basket on a chair
Or under the stairs
This treasure is covered and masked
It could be a memory from the past
It could be a diamond or a ruby rare
Yes, this is a treasure, it could be anywhere.

Daniel Leadbetter (10)
Vickerstown Primary School, Barrow-in-Furness

THE HIDDEN CASKET

Hidden away beneath the hay
Is hidden a tiny box

Only you and I know it is there
Held shut with its many locks

Nobody knows what it conceals
And it's disguised as an old tin can

Oh, look over there, what is this?
It looks like a wealthy young man

He's holding something that looks like a pin
No wait, it's a brand new hair clip

He looks through the hay and finds the box
Held shut with its many locks

He picks at the locks with his clip
Then suddenly he bites his lip

When he is done he opens the lid
And pulls out a key and a casket

He fits the key into the lock
That holds the casket shut

The items that the casket hides away
Are over a hundred years old

They are some coins from Tudor times
They are some things from a bygone age.

Scott Bartlett (10)
Vickerstown Primary School, Barrow-in-Furness

HIDDEN TREASURE

Pirate ships sailing on the sea
Dreaming of treasure like you and me

Let's dig a big hole in the sand over here
Maybe we'll find some treasure close or near

Diamonds, sapphires, rubies red
There's a splendid tiara for my head

Emeralds, amethysts, silver and gold
Precious treasures for me to hold.

Catherine Myers (11)
Vickerstown Primary School, Barrow-in-Furness

DOGGY TREASURE

As I look,
I see shining things
Right in front of my eyes.
The big, rusty, crackly box
Appears before my eyes,
Shining brightly,
In front of me.
As I opened the rusty box,
I saw my treasure,
My dog's little shadow.
It makes me feel a bit glowy,
That's my best treasure of them all.

Rebecca Conlon (8)
Willington CE Primary School, Crook

IN MY TREASURE CHEST

When I look in the wooden chest
To stop me smiling, I try my best
For things in my box are very precious
In fact, I'd say they are my treasures
A Blackpool rock from '99
I haven't eaten it, but it's still mine
A photo of my family
My sister Emma's catastrophe
A hair of my cat called Scruffy
Actually, he was quite mucky!
Right at the bottom is my first birthday card
To remember the day is very hard
Finally the buckle is closed
But now, yes still, the contents grow.

Stephen Wilson (10)
Willington CE Primary School, Crook

THE BOX

It was a rainy day,
I couldn't go out and play,
I went on an adventure in which I found,
A box complete with a pound.
There was a song which played on and on,
It stayed in my mind way too long,
But there was a coin, beautiful and round,
Which belonged to a girl who had been crowned.

Amy Hartley (11)
Willington CE Primary School, Crook

My Treasures

Going down, down and down,
Still going past the town,
Plop, in the sea,
I see a treasure chest,
Grubby and small, not really the best,
Inside, what could be there?
Cards, letters and a book,
I need a better look.
Fond memories of my family,
I must be dreaming, this is silly,
Oh look, a photo of my friends,
I never want this moment to end.
A small, purple, little pouch,
To reach it I have to crouch,
I open it up, something strange floats out,
'What are they?' I shout.
But then I realise they are memories.

Andrew Tweddle (10)
Willington CE Primary School, Crook

My Treasure Chest

I have a treasure chest with a beautiful ring,
With a special tin that echoed when I'd sing,
With rubies on the front that sparkled and shined like glowing stars
And secretly hidden chocolate bars.
In my treasure chest was my pocket money
And was I was meant to eat was my mum's home-made
disgusting honey.
My favourite dream of when I lost my magic key to unlock
my treasures.

Natalie Harker & Eliza Yeats (9)
Willington CE Primary School, Crook

IN MY DREAM

In my dream I have a place,
Where all my thoughts dance and race,
In my box my treasures stay,
Happily they are hidden away,
Try to find them you will not,
For I have the secret key to unlock.

As I sleep upon a cloud,
My thoughts keep whizzing round and round,
Inside my box you will find,
A dark blue carpet neatly lined,
As I stir, my thoughts grow clear,
Then I wake and my box must disappear.

Sarah Savage (11)
Willington CE Primary School, Crook

MY TREASURE CHEST

Inside my treasure chest,
Are the things I love best,
My memories of happy days,
Pictures of the friends I've made,
The places I've been,
The things I've seen,
A necklace from my dad,
Makes me forget the bad days I've had,
No one can see my treasure chest,
I only open it when I go to bed,
Because my treasure chest lies in my head.

Eleanor Ranson (10)
Willington CE Primary School, Crook

DOWN UNDER THE SEA

Deep under the sea,
Deep, deep down,
There might be something there like a hidden town,
The wonders still confuse me,
I'd like to find out
What could be under there.
What could be about,
A treasure chest might lie,
Under the deep blue sea,
A diver might dive down there
And find a magic tree.
So now I'm going down there,
To find out what might lie,
Way down under the sea
And under the deep blue sky.

Arron Fox (9)
Willington CE Primary School, Crook

THE TREASURE CHEST

In my dream, my chest laid,
In the place where my first sandcastle was made,
Inside the chest my memories lay,
Memories of my first birthday,
A lock of my hair that has been cut,
Now my treasure chest is shut.

Alex Woloszyn & Amy Fletcher (10)
Willington CE Primary School, Crook

TREASURE CHEST SPARKLING BRIGHT!

Treasure chest sparkling bright!
What would be my wish tonight?
My chest would have all my treasures in,
Like my dolphin keyring!
A picture of my family,
A silver brooch,
A golden coach,
A sparkling star,
A chocolate bar
Or maybe a stone,
A killer whale dome.

Treasure chest sparkling bright!
What would be my wish tonight?

Laura Louise Johnson (11)
Willington CE Primary School, Crook

TREASURE CHEST

Deep, deep down in the bottom of the ground,
I heard some strange sounds,
They were like wolves howling.

Some day I will go down
To the deep, deep ground,
At the bottom of the deep blue sea.

Amber Skelton (8) & Jaimie Simpson (9)
Willington CE Primary School, Crook

THE TREASURE CHEST

Sailing away from the land,
Pushing off from the sand,
Bobbing about on the sea,
Steering the boat is only me.
Nearing the island's bright blue bay,
Will we make it by the end of today?
Landing on the sandy shore,
On an island in the ocean's core,
Walking up towards the trees,
Only I have the keys.
Opening the treasure chest,
I find the results from my first test,
Photos of my family,
What a happy memory!

Greg Pringle (10)
Willington CE Primary School, Crook

THE TREASURE CHEST

Ocean blue, glowing bright,
Just under the aqua light,
Like waves crashing against the rocks,
The hidden wonder treasure box.
When the dolphins play
And the whales sing,
Very soon,
The box will shine in deep, dark blue.

James Edwin Lane (10)
Willington CE Primary School, Crook

AT NIGHT

At night the glittery stars will twinkle in the dark, dull,
Silent night, it will be moonlit at night.

The moon will cover the sky with its brightness,
It will also shine like a great light.

The streets are silent like a sleeping mouse.

The children are quietly tucked up in their lovely, little warm beds.

But nothing will stir at night,
Not even a mouse.
A hamster might
But that's a different matter,
If you know what I mean!

Iris Leeson (10)
Wings Of Eagles Acting School, Crosby

AN OWL

An owl is smooth, dark and silky
Glides through the air like a plane
Making no sound
He glides down to the ground
Picking some food for today
Making and mixing his food all up
He sits down on a log
'Oh, what a day'
He would say.

Courtney Wilson (9)
Wings Of Eagles Acting School, Crosby

THE FORGOTTEN CHILD

A child looked at a candle
A child safe but scared
Dim room, no door handle
A child not loved or cared

No one to share her comfort
No one at day or night
No one else in the dark room
Just her and the candlelight

She, the forgotten child
She, the no one
She, the girl that didn't exist
The girl with no life to go on.

Caitlin Johnson (10)
Wings Of Eagles Acting School, Crosby

A CHILD LOOKS AT A CANDLE

A child looks at a candle
And as he does he sees,
The whisking of the wind outside
And the movement of the trees.

A child looks at a candle,
It makes him feel so glad
And as he looks, he remembers,
The good memories he's had.

A child looks at a candle,
It makes him warm inside
And to keep that feeling with him,
He holds it by his side.

Emma McGrath (10)
Wings Of Eagles Acting School, Crosby

COULD MY STAR?

A magical wizard
May turn you into a lizard.
Could a gnome
Work a phone?
Could there ever be a dancer
Who couldn't dance?
Could there ever be an answer
And no question?
Was there ever a war
And no battle?
Was there ever a door
And no passage?
Was there ever a number
And no sum?
Was there ever somebody brainy
But dumb?
Was there ever a star
With no shine?
Did it ever belong to me
But wasn't mine?

Jenna Freeman (11)
Wings Of Eagles Acting School, Crosby